Your Path to Business Success

Your Path to Business Success

World-class entrepreneurs share business secrets for leadership success

Howard Fox

For my parents, Arlynne and Samuel Fox. Though deceased, I am continually buoyed by the love and confidence you had for me.

TABLE OF CONTENTS

ACKNOWLEDGMENTS

To all the World-Class Entrepreneurs that contributed to this book via your interviews with me on the *CEO Spotlight Radio* Podcast or the *Your Success Path Live* Facebook Livestream, you are all so amazing. There is truly something for everyone inside these pages because you said yes.

To my family and friends, especially my Aunt Eleanor, who provided the encouragement to go back to school and follow my passion for coaching.

To my coaching and leadership development peers who have joined me on the coaching journey, thank you for helping me to stretch my learning edge.

To my friends from the Sales Authenticity Mastermind, thank you for coaching me build the plane as I fly it. You ALL inspire me.

To my friends from the Sales Authenticity Success, Monday Morning, and Publish & Profit Masterminds, thank you all for your encouragement.

To my friend & mentor, Dr. Leni Wildflower, thank you for your artful mentoring & supervision. I really don't mind the 6 AM Skype calls.

A special thank you to Novelist, Joe Treasure, who accepted my vision, and who expertly brought each chapter to life with his skillful editing.

And finally, to anyone that aspires to lead, motivate, and inspire others, there is no "Easy Path" or "Silver Bullet". It can be done though, but it takes your drive to grow, make mistakes and learn from them, show humility, ask for help, get mentored, and a passion for bringing others on the journey with you.

INTRODUCTION

"Would you tell me, please, which way I ought to go from here?"

"That depends a good deal on where you want to get to," said the Cat.

"I don't much care where–" said Alice.

"Then it doesn't matter which way you go," said the Cat.

"–so long as I get SOMEWHERE," Alice added as an explanation.

"Oh, you're sure to do that," said the Cat, "if you only walk long enough."

- Lewis Carroll, *Alice's Adventures in Wonderland*, Chapter 6

Alice's conversation with the cat pretty much sums up the life of a budding business owner or entrepreneur. There is no shortage of advice about what step you should take next, or the direction you ought to go in if you don't know your way.

As a business owner and entrepreneur, I have come to appreciate the work that has gone into understanding who my ideal client is, knowing the pain they are experiencing, and drawing out from them the cost of not alleviating that pain. With this information in-hand, I become more attuned to knowing what my "best next moves" are – to get closer knowing where I want to get to, and how I can best serve my clients.

This book grew out of a series of conversations I was privileged to have with the founders of a variety of exciting and innovative business enterprises. I began interviewing business owners, entrepreneurs, coaches, and successful professionals as host of a show on CEO Spotlight Radio. Then I transitioned into Facebook with a show called *Your Success Path Live*.

I found this a great way to only have fun, but to learn about the great work being done by friends and colleagues. I reached out to my wonderful coaching network not only within the business community in my own city of Chicago but throughout the US and Canada and beyond. I found it inspiring to hear from creative individuals in the learning and development space who are making a difference in the lives of clients and customers, and to discover how they got on their various paths to success and make a difference for their own clients.

Howard Fox

My own entrepreneurial path began about eight years ago when I went back to graduate school. Like many of my interviewees, I'm a career changer. I had over 20 years as an IT business consultant and had some really bad experiences working with people that at the end of the day were not leaders. Many were managers who knew about performing tasks, but not how to lead, motivate and inspire others. Not all of them fell into that category, but enough to make me feel that I couldn't do this anymore; I needed to feel like I was making a difference for them and me. So I went back to school where I got my Masters in Leadership Development and my training as a professional coach.

I remember we took our first leadership theory course, and one assigned book was *The Leadership Challenge* by James Kouzes & Barry Posner. I started reading these pages, and it was like, oh my God, this is it, this is how to develop business owners and professionals into leaders. From there it was really pretty clear to me that it didn't matter whether you had a Harvard, Stanford or University of Michigan education. It didn't matter that you weren't born to a family of leaders. Leadership was something you could learn. It showed me I could coach clients to take the reins and learn how to develop themselves and their employees.

It clarified my thinking on what separates managers from true leaders, a question that stirs up a lot interest and debate. I think what it really comes down to is that managers know what to do, but leader knows what the right things to do are. I look at management as transactional, whereas leadership is visionary. It's modeling how things should be done. It's having a thorough understanding of your values and what it takes to bring people along, not pushing or dragging them, but leading the way.

It's crucial for people at every level in an organization to understand that organization's core values, and that springs from leadership. There has to be alignment of personal, professional, and organizational values. Without it, individuals and teams begin to cut corners for expedience sake, and then eventually cars start falling off the rails. As a leader, I think you have to continually check in with whether you're living and breathing your values. You have to continually look at yourself and your organization, and ask, how am I doing? And how are we doing? And then be open to hearing some information that maybe you might not expect to hear, but you ought to hear it anyways.

What I loved about *The Leadership Challenge* is that it was based on observable behaviors, gathered from interviews with employees and clients over more than 25 years. And they distilled leadership practices down to 30 behaviors. If you look for ways to follow these behaviors, put them into practice and commit to them, then chances are you're on a good path to move forward in leadership success. The challenges will always be there, but your compass is True North.

I also believe there's a personality perspective that needs to be looked at in leadership. I happen to be a very analytical, process driven person. You might be extroverted, action oriented, results oriented, but it just means we have different leadership styles. We can all embrace those behaviors, but we're going to put them into practice differently. That was a key takeaway from the book – that everybody, regardless of your background, can become a great leader. That includes the folks sweeping the floors, doing the maintenance, or in customer service advising customers. We all have opportunities to lead.

But leadership needs to be developed. It's important to have a mentor. I would have liked to have one earlier in life. Mentoring, in the American based model, is about "here's what I did, and if you do these things you'll be fine." This has a place, but this is not the kind of mentoring I mean. The European model of mentoring is a little different. It's much more of a coach approach. It's built on some understanding of your mentee's business, and what challenges they're facing. Find a mentor who has this familiarity with what you're going through, but will also challenge you to arrive at the decision on your own, not just tell you this is what worked for them or this is what you ought to do.

Seeking out a Mastermind is the next recommendation that I would share with a leader. There are many local, national, international organizations where you can interact with others who are in a similar leadership capacity as you. You're not going in there to solve each other's problems. You're going to learn about each other's challenges. There's a lot of benefit to discovering your blind spot. This may come from inquiring inside the organizations, asking the people who are down in the trenches, doing the work, because they may have invaluable suggestions and insights for you.

Another thing that stood out to me on the five practices of exemplary leadership is that the last practice, encouraging the heart, is the least commonly seen. The concept focuses on being sincere, including sincere celebrations devoted to recognizing employee success. That's a big thing. Survey after survey continually shows that encouraging the heart has the lowest score when staff is asked about the behaviors they observe from their leader. All organization or teams are busy, but we can't always just rely on the dollars and time metrics as a standard of success. We have to learn how to acknowledge our employees for the work they're doing and the impact it has on the bottom line. A great leader leans in and knows what their staff need in the form of encouragement.

Now when I work with leaders, there are models and instruments I find useful that support my coaching work. The DiSC instrument, the Leadership Challenge, the Five Dysfunctions of a Team, and Productive Conflict are all effective. And they go hand-in-hand, because being a great leader involves layers of complexity, including how to build teams, manage conflict, and deal with issues requiring emotional intelligence.

Leadership is complex. You have to know a lot of about the organization to begin to understand the sources of pain, to identify the problems that need to get resolved if that pain isn't to continue. This is what leadership coaching is all about.

Conflict is a huge issue. It gets to the core of who we are as humans. There's a lot of research going on in the field of neuroscience on how we can learn to manage our stress and emotions. If we're handling abrasive behavior, we tend to go into conflict because we're scared that we might not know the answer or are afraid to ask for help. We go into a fight or flight mode because we don't want to be fired or humiliated.

Helping a client to recognize what's happening when they're going into fight or flight mode, to see what's causing it, and then help them understand there are more effective ways to behave and respond – these are important components in the leadership development process. That's the beauty of an instrument like the DiSC. It helps you learn about yourself and about others at the same time. You're never going to get somebody else to change for you. You have to adapt to their needs.

If you're a leader and want to accomplish your work every day, and get things done, you have to learn how to listen, communicate, and become a credible influencer. Let your team know what you would like them to accomplish. Have good health conflict, get commitments, and then hold them accountable for achieving the results.

CHAPTER 1:

MARK KAUFMAN ON ORGANIZATION & EXECUTIVE DEVELOPMENT

Interview on CEO Spotlight Radio – April 27, 2016

Tell us something about the work that you do.

As you know, a lot of us that are in organization development or executive development, coaching, et cetera, come to this field through some type of business or career development model. Kaufman Partners has a unique mix of folks that come from both the business side and the psychology side. We're an interesting combination of former therapists, business management professionals, executive coaches. We're based in Chicago, we provide our services primarily to mid-level and executive-level folks who are either in very rapid growth mode or turnaround mode and they need a really fast combination of both talent management and business strategy.

What size company are you typically working with?

Most of my companies are mid-size and large, but I do have an individual practice where I like connecting with people one-on-one. Right now I have a global chemical company that's doing a new product release and so the focus is on innovation and transformation. I have another client that's a mid-size food manufacturing company and they're focused more on strategic alignment to a new CEO. We like to combine the achievement models of performance management with the intuitive side of change management or group process.

What are some unique challenges that you're seeing today, 2016, versus whether it's five, ten, fifteen years ago? Is there anything that's unique today that your work has evolved as a result of the workforce and the leadership of evolving?

I think all of us are always asking ourselves, "What does the market need that's different?" Right now I'm working on an article. We've been interviewing tech companies here in Chicago, everybody from Oracle to Jellyvision. Everyone knows that the rate of change is new, with this concept of market disruption, et cetera. How do we take something that was usually an annual process, the strategy, or balanced scorecard approach to management from 20, 30 years ago, and make that relevant in everyday meetings.

This article that we're writing is looking at something that Deloitte calls right speed innovation, and we've taken that word and we now call it the right speed meetings. We say, "How do we take strategic thinking that's typically redesigned every 12 months and map that onto a meeting template that is maybe changed every quarter or every six months?" Getting folks to be both strategic and intuitive at the same time in each meeting is really a new intensity in today's workplace. People want to be both more efficient and bring in more top or bottom line revenue, but are also demanding a more people-centered sense of connection. The new part is the rate of change and how we make sure people connect strategically and intuitively in every meeting and not just on an annual basis.

Executives need to get the whole system in the room. That's not a new concept. When I say the whole system, it's customers, it's clients, it's internal departments. Even though we know those most affected by change have to be part of the change process, people that are leading businesses are just so intensely focused on managing market changes that it's still a struggle to get them to break out of silos and have these whole-system meetings.

For example, the chemical company I mentioned, we have quarterly retreats where we get 12 different divisions in the room. Not only are we getting folks to talk more frequently across departments but we're also getting them to think about how they include the different people who are influencers, achievers, or connectors in their organization so that creativity and innovation, new systems and processes, are implemented one and two layers down. As intuitive as that may sound, it's just hard to do when executives get forced or pressured into being out so much more in the marketplace, working with board members or following where new customers are headed. I think it's very difficult for people who are at that executive level to slow down in order to speed up, as it were, by getting more people in the room more consistently.

I believe you're going to have one of the icons of organization development coming to Chicago soon.

As you know, I'm the board chair of the Chicago Organization Development Network. One of our members Maggie Shreve, along with Emily Axelrod, was able to get Edgar Schein to come to town. Everyone in our field that has done organization development knows that Edgar Schein was one of the original thinkers around organization culture. One of his first books is called Process Consultation, which is a fancy way of saying what people nowadays call candid conversations or courageous conversations. Edgar is a professor emeritus I believe at MIT and he's worked with many global companies around how you identify the cultural values, and the cultural stories, and the different cultural rituals that play out at different key events for organizations. How do you manage that, whether it's through assessments, or getting people in the room, or redesign, or any number of things?

Mark Kaufman, lead practitioner in organization effectiveness and leadership development, helps executives and management teams come together to achieve:

- *Next Level Leadership Development*

- *Innovation Mindset Teams*

- *Right Speed Meetings*

- *Pre and Post Merger & Acquisition Alignment*

Mark's expertise is in connecting business strategy to people strategy. He connects quickly, engages divergent points of views and manages creative tension when teams are designing or vying for position when developing talent management solutions. Mark is trained to gather performance improvement and people data to make sure groups identify next levels of growth and measurable steps to get there.

YOUR NEXT STEPS

To learn more about Mark and his work, visit his website at www.Kaufman-Partners.com.

You can also contact Mark a Mark@Kaufman-Partners.com, and connect with him on LinkedIn at:
https://www.linkedin.com/in/markkaufman2/

CHAPTER 2:

DR. LARRY GARD ON HIRING & SUCCESSION PLANNING

Interview on CEO Spotlight Radio – April 27, 2016

I would love if you could share with our guests a little bit about the work that you do and the work of Hamilton Chase Consulting.

Hamilton Chase, I like to say, focuses on both ends of the work spectrum from hiring to retiring. I specialize in working with smaller businesses on the hiring process – whether it's refining their interviews, learning to ask better questions, learning what constitutes a good answer, or sometimes introducing psychological testing as part of their hiring process – to make sure that it's a really good fit on both sides.

At the opposite end of the extreme, I work with either career professionals or business owners who are thinking of stepping away from full-time work to focus on the head and heart aspects of that huge life transition. For many Americans, depending upon their health, the post work period, whether you call it retirement or whatever label you want to use for it, could be one of the longest phases of life. It's more than just about saving money. You have to give a great deal of thought to what that period is going to be like.

What are some of the challenges for a career professional getting ready to walk away and plan that next stage of their life?

It has the potential to be an emotionally disruptive period and even if it's not disruptive, it's still pronounced. Whether you're a CEO or an entrepreneur who's been running the firm, there are all kinds of changes that stepping away can introduce. You'll be leaving a familiar role. There may be a shift in status. You may have a significant change in your daily routine or how your week is structured. And you may lose many of the rewards that you used to associate with your work, whether it's the feelings of accomplishment, a feeling of being in charge, a sense of purpose for your daily activities, and relationships you've had with your peers and your employees, clients, vendors. There's also the issue of legacy. How will you be remembered and for how long? What will happen to the firm once you leave? Lots of big issues arise.

It seems like this takes time and effort, and the longer you plan for it the better.

Without question. You're talking about a huge transition and a huge change in your daily routine. And yet I think most people spend more time planning their kitchen renovation or their daughter's wedding or deciding what new set of golf clubs to buy than they do psychologically preparing for this period of their life. Certainly we see the disruption that can occur in companies. When I've been doing executive coaching, I've had HR people come to me and say, "Hey Larry, while you're here, we have this vice president – they've been with us a long time and we've had some initial chats about when they might want to step down but they won't give us a firm answer. They won't make a decision. This is really creating some questions for us as a company because, if we can't get a firm answer on when they'll be leaving, it means that we can't give a firm response to the people behind them with regard to when they might be getting a promotion. It's tough to make decisions about whether or not to take on certain projects because we don't know if this person will be here or in the process of leaving and we're concerned. What if they agree to step down but they won't step away?"

I've heard of situations where, because the executive hasn't sorted through this in their own mind and it comes on very suddenly, they won't really cooperate with the succession plan. They'll criticize or undermine their successor. It is absolutely critical that a good deal of thought be given to it.

Is there one model for this, or is everything is on a case-by-case basis?

There are some tools out there for approaching this but, as a life transition, I think it's one of those areas where we do feel very much on our own. It's not like when we were going off to college, when we might have had a college counselor or a parent or an older sibling or an older cousin to show us the ropes or tell us what we might expect. Many people facing retirement feel very much like they're on their own. Now they may see some of their friends going through it, but everybody's situation is different. The psychological aspects of it tend to be unique for each individual.

A lot of times people's expectations stem from what they saw a parent or a grandparent go through. We sometimes see this with business owners. They insist that they're going to work until they die at their desk because they saw what happened to their father, their grandfather. Of course, those old messages are hard to break through, but they're limiting.

Is there a book that you'd recommend for somebody who's starting to contemplate this?

There is a book by Jack Beauregard, it's available through a website called The Platinum Years. I believe it's called *What's Next?*

The other thing I would say is that leaders want to ask themselves, how do you want to be remembered? As a resolute, unyielding commander who died at your desk because you didn't want to relinquish authority. As an amiable but out of touch founder of the company, who does more harm than good because you aren't willing to empower the next generation? Or do you want to be remembered as a thoughtful leader who put the needs of the company ahead of your own ego, providing sound stewardship?

Dr. Larry Gard *is a consulting psychologist with over 20 years of experience helping people overcome the all-too-human obstacles that impede performance and profitability. He heads Hamilton-Chase Consulting, a Chicago-based firm that focuses on workplace issues from hiring to retiring.*

YOUR NEXT STEPS

To learn more about Dr. Gard and his work, visit his website at www.hamiltonchaseconsulting.com

You can also contact Dr. Gard at drlgard@hamiltonchaseconsulting.com, or connect with him on LinkedIn at https://www.linkedin.com/in/drlarrygard.

CHAPTER 3:

AMANDA NEELY ON MISSION-BASED ENTREPRENEURSHIP

Interview on CEO Spotlight Radio – May 25, 2016

Tell us a bit about the Overflow Coffee Bar and how you've set this up because I think it's very unique.

Overflow Coffee Bar is more than just your typical coffee shop. We are a space for the community and we're changing the world one cup at a time. We like to bring people together to both change the world globally through how the products we use are sourced and making sure farmers and whatnot are paid well for their hard work. And we're changing the world locally through this community of people that have come together here in the South Loop at our location. We're also changing the city through economic development. We're actually a social enterprise, a low-profit LLC, organized for a social mission prior to making a profit.

How did community centric vision for the Overflow come about? Or what led you to say, "This is what we want to do?"

I'm a millennial, so changing the world and being optimistic is in my DNA or in my generation. The roots of what we're doing trace back to me watching Save The Whale documentaries when I was a kid and forcing my parents to recycle. There's a large movement going on of people who want to do good while doing well, and don't have to sacrifice the well-being of others in order to make money. My husband and I heard the rumblings of this. We said, "Well, this is how our business should be." And we just went down that rabbit trail and this was how it brought us the coffee that we use.

How do you source your product and find your staff?

It's called direct-trade. We cut out a ton of middlemen. There's usually about seven or eight different middlemen, each taking their cut from the coffee farmer to the end consumer. So the coffee farmer gets very little. Instead with our coffee, our friend Tim Taylor who's up in Bucktown, in the northwest side of Chicago, goes and works directly with the coffee farmers, arranges for the export and import of the coffee into the United States, and then he roasts it right there in Bucktown. We get it the next day and we sell it directly to the customer. It's nice and fresh, too.

When we're hiring, we very much put forward that we're a social enterprise and a socially responsible coffee shop. And that tends to attract a different kind of potential barista to apply to work here. They're often choosing to apply here because they already believe in what we're doing and they want their work to matter. So we typically are attracting other millennials that are activists. They're doing volunteer activities and trying to change the world and this is going to fit into that part of their life. It's also really helped us with retention because the people who work here feel like they are making a difference and they're less likely to move on to a different job because they feel like this has more value than just a paycheck.

What's changing as a result of the Overflow Coffee Bar in the community?

As we looked at our neighborhood and how we can make a difference here, what we realized is that a lot of businesses are struggling in the South Loop. It was the fastest growing neighbourhood in the nation in 2007, so tons of residents moved in here, but businesses have been slow to follow, partly because of the recession of 2008, 2009. But also partly because a lot of places were built and our population went from zero to ten or twenty thousand people. But compared to other neighborhoods in Chicago that have forty or eighty thousand people, there's just not the density here. So, it's harder to have a healthy business.

A great opportunity for us, as an anchor in the neighbourhood, is to help the other businesses grow, to build community amongst the businesses, to provide more jobs and make this a thriving, vigorous neighbourhood. That's good for the south side of Chicago, but also for all of Chicago. So that's where we've taken our local mission.

What's been the challenge or lessons learned when it comes to finding the right people that are aligned with your passion and your mission?

Rule number one of Overflow – and with every employee this is one of the first things they hear on their first day – is "communicate, communicate, communicate." That's been really great for us, especially working with younger employees. They'll send me text messages to let me know this or that. When something's going wrong we'll talk about it rather than push it under a rug. I try to model that and make sure that I'm always over-communicating. I've gotten great responses from our staff and they've over-communicated back to me and that's just really helped us in all kinds of great and not-so-great situations.

Now we're looking at opening a second location, here in Chicago, somewhere. We're starting to put together our business plan for that and to look for prime locations. Of course, that will come with its own challenges with hiring managers and training them and we'll have to communicate even better.

What are you doing to continue to develop yourself?

For my own learning and development, I love podcasts. Actually, I have a three or four, maybe five now, that I listen to when I go to the gym or when I'm walking to the bank or that kind of thing. Usually the podcasts will send me to other things, like books to read or websites to check out or tools that I might use. It doesn't actually take any of my time. I'm doing it while I'm doing something that's also good for me.

Amanda Neely is co-founder and co-owner of Overflow Coffee Bar, L3C. Amanda and her husband opened Overflow Coffee Bar in 2011 as a social enterprise focused on achieving a social mission prior to making a profit. Amanda is a knowledgeable entrepreneur with experience in creatively solving the challenges inherent to growing and starting a business.

YOUR NEXT STEPS

To learn more about Amanda and her work, she loves to share her experiential knowledge as a certified life and business coach through overflowyourpossibility.com. If you're interested in a free Strategy Session with Amanda, you can sign-up at www.overflowyourpossibility.com/successpath.

You can also connect with Amanda on LinkedIn at www.linkedin.com/in/amandaneely/, Facebook at www.facebook.com/OverflowCoffeeBar/, and Twitter at www.twitter.com/overflowamanda.

CHAPTER 4:

MIKE PALESTINA & MAGGIE PAZIAN ON EMOTIONAL INTELLIGENCE

Interview on CEO Spotlight Radio – July 6, 2016

Please introduce yourselves and what you do.

Maggie: My background is in academia. I brought knowledge around the science and psychology of non-verbal communication and emotions and how that manifests in behavior into training programs and the coaching that we do as part of People Intell Institute. We focus on leadership development and we apply the science and the concept of self-awareness, self-management, social awareness, and relationship management into our practice in developing leaders and delivering training programs.

Mike: With Maggie's unique background in the science of emotions and my almost thirty year career in corporate America with a variety of leadership roles, we formed People Intell. The combination of her skills and mine, and the fact that we offer a triad model for coaching where Maggie and I are both in the room with each of our clients, has been working very well for the last three plus years.

Maggie: As you can imagine, organizations are made up of different personalities. People are so different. At the same time, there's drive, there's motivation, and things that we all look for in terms of feeling fulfilled. One of the key things that we believe in is that relationships are at the core of everything you do, whether it is in a corporate environment or not – relating to other people, understanding what makes them tick, managing ourselves in a way that we can work with people in a dynamic situation. We use all these skills to bring self-awareness. First and foremost, you need to be self-aware in order to build the foundation to great leadership and great relationships. You're looking at things like having self-control, developing trustworthiness, conscientiousness, adaptability, innovation.

Mike: The vast majority of our clients are high potential, high performing employees at whatever level within an organization. We have the luxury of working with those folks. They've already established a trajectory for themselves that's working very well. They recognize, or someone has recognized for them, that there are things they need to work on, to enhance, in order to get to the next level and be successful at that point. We all have things that we need to improve. We all have things that maybe we need to stop doing. We get to work with really outstanding employees to begin with. Every once and a while, we'll get an engagement that's more of a remedial type of situation. Fortunately, we don't get that very often, and, fortunately, more and more employers are using coaching less and less in remedial situations. We get to work with the superstars. Again, it could be at the C level or down to entry-level supervisory folks. Because we don't have to help them make major changes in who they are functionally, we focus on behaviors. There are some derailing behaviors that we all have and we work with folks over the course of six or nine months, focused very much on one or two things that they want to address over that time frame. We identify those objectives as a group. Their sponsoring supervisor will be involved, human resources will be involved, our client will certainly be involved.

How does a client find you?

Mike: Well, to date, and we see this not changing at all going forward, it has been through personal equity. Maggie and I each have a lot of experience and robust networks and we've reached out to folks that we've known over the years, explained what we were doing when we first started out, and then the domino effect. We have a nice core group of customers, employers, that we go back to with recurring business. We seem to be breaking ground with new employers almost quarterly, where Maggie will know someone or I'll know someone, we'll make the call and say, "Hey, can we come on in and talk a little bit about what we're trying to achieve?" We were at an employer last year. They were nice enough to invite us in for a half an hour discussion. When we told them what we focused on, the person that we were meeting with just shot back in her chair and said, "We have that problem. Who doesn't have that problem?" It's just been word of mouth and then, once we get in a room with folks, it seems to resonate.

How does your program differ from others?

Maggie: Mike and I both believe that staying on top of research and implementing new findings into the trainings is really important. The workshops we create are typically modular. We deliver them over a longer period of time to support more sustainable retention and change across the folks attending. One of the things we know is that, if you attend a one-time training, a lot of times you walk out, everything is great, you're excited about the information, but it doesn't translate into change for most people. We look at how to make this more sustainable. That's key for us. We want folks who walk out of that room with new knowledge to be able to use it, to apply it, and to form new habits, so they can start to develop and grow into their potential.

What are some of the challenges leaders are finding and how are you working with them?

Mike: What's basic across most engagements is, as folks work their career and ascend up the corporation, there's more and more pressures on delivering whatever it is that they're there to deliver. They have direct reports, they have numbers. If they get up into the C level, they've got board reports. We tend to find, and research backs this up, that, once you hit a certain level, you forget some of what you know about behaviors because you're so distracted and stressed. After you hit a mid-level manager or director level in a typical organization, you start to come down in terms of using your EQ in your day-to-day interactions. The research shows that, and that seems to be our experience, as well.

Maggie: What gets the middle managers and directors to their level is actually high emotional intelligence scores. They are the ones that tend to stand out in those qualities. Yet the higher up you go towards the CEO level, emotional intelligence scores tend to drop. There's less emotional intelligence within the C suite. What we see is, then, challenges from a behavioral perspective because we lose those skills and abilities. It's not like riding a bike, where you learn how to ride it, and then twenty years go by, you get back on the bike, and you can ride it again – you don't forget. Emotional intelligence and the skills that are involved in that are more like learning to play an instrument. If you stop practicing, you won't retain that same level as you would if you kept practicing day after day. That's what you have to do with emotional intelligence. You have to incorporate it into your day-to-day life, into your day-to-day decision making and behaviors and thought processes. The CEOs who are the most successful in organizations have the highest emotional intelligence. While emotional intelligence goes down as you go up the ladder, those that are most successful have the highest scores.

What leads a C level executive to get involved with your work?

Mike: In the perfect scenario, it's self-awareness. They realize they have areas that they need to work on, and then they seek that help. More often than not, though, it's someone else, a trusted advisor, a direct report who is a senior level executive with a successful career. Their chief HR officer is usually the source, whispering in their ear saying, "You might want to focus on this. You might want to work on this a little bit more." But the perfect scenario is they've come upon it themselves.

How do you know that the process is working for them?

Mike: When you're talking about behaviors, it's through observation, it's through insights from other folks. Let's step back for a second. We talk about working with high potential, high performing folks, but we still look for three key things within those folks when we're called in to have a discussion. The first is awareness, whether it's self-awareness or that someone whispered in their ear. The second is a sense of urgency. They don't want to wait until the end of the quarter or when they get back from vacation. They want to start working on it today. The third is vulnerability, which is a key element of leadership. They're willing to have us speak to a variety of folks that they interact with on a daily basis in a confidential way to hear what other people are thinking about their leadership style. If we get those three things, we know we're going to be successful at the end of an engagement because they're already there. Now, we just need to plot the course. It does come down to observations of others and how our clients feel about themselves. The confidence level starts to build almost immediately. We don't leave a discussion without providing practical, applicable techniques for when they walk out of their office. They can start doing something that we talk about immediately.

How has it been for you two working together?

Maggie: I think it's been easy. When we started we were basically two strangers. We met a couple times and it felt right and we decided to give it a try. The last few years have been huge growth from my perspective, having learned so much from Mike with his experience and his background. Hopefully, I'm giving back as well from my experience and my background. In many ways, we couldn't be more different in cultural background. I'm originally from Poland. I grew up in Montreal, Canada, finally came to the US in my teenage years. English is my third language. Mike was born in Newark, New Jersey, and grew up here. But we have the same passion, we have fairly similar values, and I think that's what has brought us together in terms of how we work together and why we are so successful.

Mike: It's simple from my perspective. I am an incredibly lucky human being. I feel Maggie and I met strictly through serendipity. On a trip to London, someone introduced me to a colleague of his from Manchester, UK. I had a Skype call with that gentleman a couple of weeks after I got back, and he said, "There's this woman, Maggie Pazian, that you need to meet." And Maggie and I lived within an hour of each other. I had to go over to London to meet someone right up the road here. Serendipity had a big part of it, luck has a big part of it. I would agree 100% with Maggie that it has been easy. We had a chemistry that just flowed immediately. What's really nice is, in almost every evaluation we get, people will mention the chemistry between us. We did nothing to cultivate that, it just happened.

Mike Palestina is a Certified Executive Coach and Leadership Development Consultant who collaborates with senior executives, mid-level managers, and other leaders to inspire and enhance individual attitudes, behaviors, and performance, resulting in increased employee engagement and retention. These shifts ultimately contribute to successfully reaching desired goals and exceeding individual and organizational expectations.

Mike is passionate about helping others modify behaviors. He blends coaching practices with mentoring, advising, and counseling as well, thus providing his clients with a richer interpersonal experience in which to modify attitudes, behaviors, and performance.

Maggie Pazian is an internationally accredited expert in the science and art of nonverbal communication and behavior, emotion perception and deception detection. She has more than ten years of experience coaching and training others in the skills of accurately perceiving and interpreting emotional information. By drawing upon the scientifically validated five channels of communication and using the Facial Action Coding System and micro expression analysis, she is able to guide others in the process of becoming more emotionally aware and connected. Enhanced emotional awareness allows for better decision-making, stronger leadership, and more effective relationships. Maggie is committed to helping leaders grow and evolve in this area.

YOUR NEXT STEPS

To learn more about Mike & Maggie's work, and Executive Coaching – Team and Leadership Development at the People Intell Institute, call them at 973-534-8685, or visit their website at www.people-intell.com.

CHAPTER 5:

ELINA GIACHALI ON NEURO-LINGUISTIC PROGRAMMING

Interview on CEO Spotlight Radio – July 27, 2016

Tell us a little bit more about your background and what is NLP?

A few things about me. I started a studying from a marketing premise when I was younger. But it is when you don't know much about who you are, where you want to go. So you just try and pick a safe choice. And it seemed that life guided me where I belonged. And I soon acquired my own business.

By the time I was in my late twenties, I had a school of my own. And I had the opportunity to practice both my business skills and my marketing skills, both leadership and the skills to do with the human resources, with motivation of people. How to help them achieve their goals when it comes to doing well in exams, overcoming their fears. So, again one led to the other and I soon found out that I didn't want to go on working with children anymore and I stepped forward to work with adults. Because my own children had become adults and wanted me to guide them in their next phase in life. So I started working on how to guide them, to culture them, in their path to success. And this is a small introduction to how I ended up being a life and business coach. I have been practicing for the last six years now.

What are some challenges you are seeing and how is NLP helping?

I started working with stress management and with NLP. NLP is a method that gives you an opportunity to use your own mind to your own benefit. There are a lot of exercises that were inspired by people we are coaching, athletes for the Olympic Games, to have a winner's mentality. When I was coaching my children to success, I soon found out that the strongest students were the ones that would fail the test. The most skilled students would fail due to their stress. And of course, we have skilled professionals in the corporate environment or entrepreneurs who are highly skilled and have a great idea and are well trained, but don't do well because of their own inner critic, their own inner limits.

What is the origin of that inner critic and how do we get past that?

You can overcome the barrier. This is what happens when you do some coaching. When you do some work with yourself. In business, it is a blessing when you find yourself out of your comfort zone. I believe that it is a real blessing to be out of your comfort zone every now and then. Which means that something is really happening, something bigger than what you were expecting. So it is quite natural and quite human for people to have a bit more stress, a louder inner criticism than they can handle. Once they go back to their inner strength, once they are tuned with their best self, with their values, once they are tuned with their higher mission, then it stops being about their own performance. Because what we are doing as leaders, we are not doing for us. We are doing it for the people. We are doing it to offer service.

Do children get that concept more quickly than adults?

We can trick children easier because all a child needs to have is an adult that believes in them. When I said to my students,

"You can do it, it's a piece of cake for you," then they actually condition their minds to go do it. And the same thing happened with my teachers, my personnel. When they motivated their students, their students believed. Because children – we have a phrase here in Greece – they have small external gods. So once you say they are bad, they believe they are bad. Once you say they are good – "you can do it, it's a piece of cake" – then they go do it. With adults this changes, because adults think that they know better.

As kids we learn from everybody around us. What is it about those challenges that make them more difficult for us as adults?

When you are a child, you experiment with what is right and what is wrong, what works and what doesn't. But when we are exposed by our parents or by our environment, or even by our teachers, to information that is wrong about what we can do or what we can't, this becomes a limiting belief. And those limiting beliefs, when we grow up, we make them law. They become our personal laws of life.

For example, some person may have a personal law that they will never find a perfect customer, there is no such thing as a perfect customer, or there is no such thing as my ideal job, or there is no such thing as working in a job that makes me feel complete. And there are a lot of people that actually believe that the work has to be something which is compulsory and a little bit unpleasant. It's something mandatory and we have to sacrifice some of our time and then go on back to our life. Which is never the case. I believe that people should find their personal mission in life. Because what happens is that others need them. So what can they do best?

In the States we have a "do whatever it takes" attitude. It's always about getting things done. And I think that does us a disservice, because if we can first be clear on our mission we can start to work more effectively. How do people discover what their mission is?

When it comes to leadership, the leader definitely has to be aware of his mission. Otherwise, he can't lead himself first. We have the "do whatever you can" mentality in Greece too. But we take it from the wrong edge. We take it from the edge of do whatever you can to be successful, or do whatever you can to make a living, or do whatever you can to make money, to create wealth. I believe that it should be do whatever you can to find what makes you tick. And then also to be of service to people. The money, wealth, living, will follow. So I believe strongly that this is what we must focus on. We must find what is the field where we are indispensable.

This is a reality for me, and for a lot of my clients, because the drive, the energy, the power, the motivation follows. You wake up earlier. You get informed about everything. When you have found your big love, what you are made to do, the drive is immense. And the magnet follows, the magnet of the perfect client. The magnet of the perfect income. The ideal. Because let's not use the word perfect, there is no perfection and that's the perfection. The ideal client will follow, the ideal income will follow, the ideal lifestyle will follow when you have found your real love. I have worked with people that came to me with a gray look, a gray shadow over their eyes. And once they found what makes them tick, they actually became like 10 or 15 years younger. They started working harder and being a lot less tired.

What does that moment of insight look like for that leader?

It's like a rebirth. And people tend to forget what happened in the past. It's as if their life has always been like that. They become a lot more lively.

And I imagine the people who work for the leader, even the family, they see something different about him.

First of all, he's happier. Second, he's more serene. Even if he needs to work more hours. And there's fulfillment. We came into this life to be fulfilled, not to make money. Money is a means. We have confused the means with the end destination. We came in this life to feel fulfilled, to feel serene, to make ourselves and our loved ones happy. We didn't come into this life to accumulate money and then spend it in a very expensive hospital, where we will treat the illnesses that have accumulated in our body because we have been maltreating it, because we have been coping with stuff that we didn't want to cope with for too long.

Elina Giachali is a NLP Life & Business Coach, Speaker and Entrepreneur. She is a Certified NLP Master Practitioner and Social and Emotional Coach. She has been teaching and training people for more than 15 years. She has been coaching them towards their own path to success for more than 6. She has spoken to crowds of over 100 people giving numerous speeches per year. She is a result-oriented individual, very competent with realizing how the others are driven to their path towards change and what they need to know that particular moment. What drives them to unstuck from their own stuckness. She takes into consideration various factors and various tools when she is designing her course of action, her speeches and seminar plans. From down to earth Marketing and Life Coaching tools to NLP, Greek Philosophy, Motivational Psychology, Neuroscience and the more spiritual Meditation.

YOUR NEXT STEPS

To learn more about Elina and her work, visit her website at www.lifecoachelina.com. You can also contact Elina at elina@lifecoachelina.com, or connect with her on LinkedIn at: www.linkedin.com/in/elina-giachali-83315330/

CHAPTER 6:

DIANE HALFMAN ON ORGANIZING YOUR PHYSICAL SPACE

**Interview on CEO Spotlight Radio –
October 26, 2016**

*Share a little bit about yourself and your
background. What is the Diane Halfman
Academy?*

Something you may not know
about me is that I was a police officer
with the San Diego Police Department
for ten years. Unfortunately I was
badly injured in a training accident
and was forced to medically retire far too soon.

During my time at the police department I worked as first a
uniformed patrol officer and I also worked several undercover
assignments in gangs, narcotics and vice. I saw people at their
worst and their best. During my time as a cop I was literally in
thousands of homes, and I noticed something early on and it was
confirmed repeatedly during my career. The homes that had the
most clutter had the most drama. I call this the clutter to drama
ratio. It's directly proportional. The ratio goes both ways. If you
have a lot of drama in your life you probably have a lot of clutter,
and if you have a lot of clutter you end up with a lot of drama.

What prompted you to become an entrepreneur?

When I retired from the department I had a passion to support people in their personal environments, since I saw so many environments that weren't working for people. I wanted to continue to serve them. Helping people up-level their environments has brought my clients tremendous financial success, but more importantly it's brought them the happiness and joy of living the way that they want.

Bringing awareness to them is a big thing because lots of times people don't see that their environment can lead to the drama in their life. As they start realizing how much impact our environment has, a lot of people think they can have the willpower, like "I can just clear this out and everything will be okay." It's even in your kitchen. Let's say that you want to have a healthy diet but you don't have healthy things in there. Well you can have all the willpower you want but in the middle of the night, if that cupcake is there, you're probably going to eat it. If you create an environment that either doesn't have cupcakes or has inspiring things in it, you're going to win.

How do they get to the point where they can say they need help?

Usually something happens in their life. They hit a crisis point, unfortunately. Usually people don't just wake up in the morning and go, "I want to clear out my clutter." Sometimes they do realize they can't get their hands on what they need when they need it, and as an entrepreneur, if you can't find your resources in a timely matter it can actually affect your credibility. You can also be overwhelmed. Sometimes people are moving an office, or downsizing at home, and they realize it's just time to look at it.

What happens with entrepreneurs sometimes is that each day things just start to pile up. We look around and realize that we haven't looked through the mail for weeks and we haven't put some filing away. Maybe we haven't gotten the support in our office to help us. Then people get to the point where they're sometimes a little embarrassed that somebody actually sees their space because it doesn't really reflect who they are. Wanting somebody who will support them, won't judge them, and know that they just need some systems, will spur people to finally make a phone call.

So when you start to work with your clients, what's the first step?

I typically have an interview with them to find out where they're at and what support they need. Some people are self-starters and just need some guidance. Some people want to have the VIP experience where they work with me one-on-one. I have a yearlong mentorship program for my VIPs where I personally help them get their life under control. I also have two online courses for clients who like the more do-it-yourself approach.

With my Diane Halfman Academy, I have two courses. One is my Clutter to Calm course for the entrepreneur who wants to tackle many different areas of their life. They're good when they get a blueprint and can do it on their own, with some guidance and support. I also have my Paper Clutter Solution program. This is for the client who just needs to get un-buried from all the paper in their lives. This course gives them a simple structure where they know exactly what to do with each piece of paper as it lands in their hands. It's important not to just get organized, but stay organized, and my system gives you the tools to do that.

Because we all have different ways we like to learn, as well as audio my academy has very short videos, anywhere from five to fifteen minutes. I also have some download checklists that makes it easy for people to follow my five-step system.

Can you share some examples of clients, the work you've done, and the impact it's had?

I work with high achieving entrepreneurs and I guide them in getting rid of chaos in their lives. I specialize in working with people who have attained success in their work, but the rest of their life is out of alignment. I've worked with a celebrity health coach who wasn't feeling very healthy, which made her feel out of integrity. So we scaled down and cleared out over forty years of clutter. After working with her and her team, her productivity increased significantly. It brought more order to her office. She was able to have peace of mind. .

I also worked with a branding and image consultant managing the different personalities in her family, because a lot of entrepreneurs work out of their home. To create clear boundaries between office space versus family space, I designed systems for her that the whole family could buy into. She'd told me she felt lighter, had better focus, was sleeping better, and was able to communicate better with her team because she could find what she was looking for in a timely manner.

Do you help people with one bedroom condos?

I do. And it's funny because in a smaller space a lot of times people think: "Well, I have a smaller space, I've got less to deal with." But you think of all the different hats that we wear in our lives, whether we're spending time as an entrepreneur, being in our kitchens, sleeping. Even if it's in one space, you want to designate different areas where you're having the experience that you want. It's not just about having tidy piles on your desk. It's how does it feel in your space and how is it functioning for you so that it's a reflection of the life that you want to live?

In the area where you sleep you want it to feel calm. If there's paper under your bed, you're probably not resting well. When you're wanting to relax you want to have that comfy chair in a place where you can maybe read or wind down. It's really about how you want to feel in the space, and how does it support you.

I imagine that when an entrepreneur works with you there's a positive impact on the whole team.

Absolutely. Even if you're a leader of one, you still have a team. There's still people you connect with and collaborate with. A lot of times people say, "Oh I can work in the chaos. It's fine. I can find everything I need." But even if it takes you an extra five to ten minutes to find something, time is our biggest asset. If you can't find what it is you're looking for then you're not able to delegate. How many times do you hear entrepreneurs go, "I don't need anyone to help me because it's faster for me to find something myself." If you're saying that, it's code for clutter. You can't delegate it because you can't find it. And then you can't create systems, and you can't build up your business. When you're organized, you set that tone for your team. They feel more calm in their space and they're more productive.

I host these luxury retreats that allow people to get away and experience what it feels like to be in an environment that feels good and supports you. My clients come away not only rejuvenated, but with a renewed focus on the important areas of their life, a focus on happiness, health, and wealth. As entrepreneurs, sometimes we're just focusing on our business and we're not looking at how we can balance out the other areas of our life. They come away with new tools and systems that propel them towards success.

A lot of times if people are living in that chaos and business and clutter, they either forget or have never experienced what it's like to be in an environment that supports them, so the retreats support them in having that experience and learning how to take those tools home. And a lot of times I custom make retreats for teams, so people will create a retreat around their team members and really hit home some of the systems to support all of them.

What impact has it had on you since you made this career change?

For one, it's great to be an entrepreneur. I love the entrepreneurial spirit where you get to create the life you want to live. You don't have an income ceiling. And then you have a direct impact on people, that's the greatest reward. Even people who are retired from business, who don't want to have their family have to look through their things. For me to kind of be a kind of confidant, working hand in hand with them, that's the greatest reward.

Diane Halfman *is an industry speaker on organizing your physical spaces for optimal productivity and excellence. She shares this through a concept she calls "SpaLife", recreating the feeling of walking into a spa into your everyday life; that Ahh, rejuvenating, calm and serenity experience. She helps create an ideal environment that supports her clients' goals and inspires them to be at their best.*

Diane offers SpaLife Retreats, where her clients experience how to create your SpaLife through 9 distinct elements. Her signature talk is the "3 steps to creating a workspace that makes you more productive and profitable". She facilitates two virtual courses: Clutter to Calm and The Paper Clutter Solution, and she hosts VIP Days: Creating your SpaLife living space from de-cluttering to creating systems and structures for more balance and productivity.

Diane's diverse credentials serve her clients with passion and practicality. She has served as police officer, is an Ultimate Game of Life Certified coach, and holds Master's degree in Human Resources Management with an emphasis on structure and systems. Giving back is at the core of Diane's work. 10% of her sales go to charities with a focus on women and children's health.

YOUR NEXT STEPS

To learn more about Diane and her work, visit her website at www.DianeHalfman.com. You can contact Diane at Diane@DianeHalfman.com. You can also connect with Diane on LinkedIn at LinkedIn.com/in/dianehalfman; on Facebook at DianeHalfmanFan, and on Twitter at @DianeHalfman.

Diane also invites you to visit TheClutterAwarenessQuiz.com to take the Clutter Awareness Quiz.

Chapter 7:

Satori Mateu on Peak Performance

Interview on CEO Spotlight Radio – Nov. 16, 2016

Share a bit about your background and your programs.

When I was 21 years old I was pretty low in my

life, at the very bottom, so the contrast is completely different. When I was 21 years old I was about to commit suicide, and I think that's probably the lowest of self-worth you could possibly have in that moment. Obviously I didn't do it. I'm here. But I in '94 I moved to the United States from Sweden and within 6 months of that time I became world champion in Karate. I had been training in Karate since I was 6 years old, but I hadn't done it for a long time, and having made a decision, I wanted to really accomplish something of significance.

I became world champion. I opened my own martial arts school and at that point in '95 that's when I met Tony Robbins the first time and decided that this is what I want to do, I want to help people in transforming their lives, their businesses. I sought out who I thought were the best people in the world at what they were doing, at creating transformation, creating change. From that moment I decided to work on increasing people's wealth.

What I mean by that is genuine wealth. I look at your ability to access your inner and outer resources at the highest level, how you can optimize those things to really activate the best in you. That's how the journey started.

I've trained many people, high performers, in many different arenas and that got me to see how a lot of times as a high performer you have certain façade, a certain persona that you need to have to the world. The other side of that is that we have other traits that show up. If we don't deal with them, we'll have imbalance and conflict. It's important to make sure we integrate them and are congruent in our message. That's what I got to see when I created my programs. People have a certain way of being and when they can't uphold that they beat themselves up, they judge themselves. With that, they lower their own value.

Do you work with a coach, to help you to stay sharp in your game?

Absolutely, I do have mentors and coaches. Today, everybody and their mom is a coach, so it's really hard to identify someone that has quality and produces results. That's why I define them more as a mentor and I look at what are the results that they produce. Are they actually implementing it in their own lives? I pay a lot of money for my mentors, not that money in itself would make a difference. The truth is that, when you have someone that has spent 10, 15, 20 years or more to really master their craft, I really want to be able to compress that time and use their knowledge and expertise, so I can get the most out of it.

When I wanted to become a world champion in Karate, I sought out the best martial arts master in the world and personally trained with him. When I wanted to learn business skills I sought out the best of the best in business. Whether it personal development, or love, or physical health. I always look for people that had a real history of producing results. That's really the key.

Who are your ideal clients and how do they go about working with you?

I look at the kind of qualities they have because sometimes people look for quick fixes. They have a fantasy of what they want. I think that anybody that is in any kind of entrepreneurial field must want to accomplish something. You see somebody, let's say, with a great physical body, they're in great shape, and you look at them and you have this fantasy and you say, "I want to look like that." But you don't want to take the necessary actions or choose the habits that that person has. You don't see the commitment, or the relentless pursuit they had to achieve that, the rejections and the work that they put in to it. I look for people that have something they really want and are committed to the action that is required to get there. They're hungry, they're willing to have that consistent ritual to get what they want.

They're willing to make the investment, to expend the time, the energy, the resources to achieve that goal.

Yes. Like there are two seasons of success, the season of sowing and the season of reaping. Everybody who breaks through financially puts in the time for sowing. Not every thing you are going to do is going to be fun at first. But you get to learn to love the challenge, because when you learn to love the challenge, you'll be supported, you'll grow and you'll prosper. Most people look for a life that is supported and easy, and is going to be smooth. Which is why people look for that next shiny object. When you see a brilliant performance by an actor, or musician, or an athlete, or someone doing amazing things in business, you're seeing an end result, you're seeing the reaping. You're not seeing the sowing – the determination, the obsession, the disappointment, or the criticism that went to get the results. Masters make it look easy. And that's the different between living in a fantasy and actually being hungry to get the result.

I'll give you an example. I had a client that I worked with not that long ago. She's an international trainer, she's a natural at networking. She used to have a workshop where she charged $250. I said to her you're completely devaluing yourself. So we created a back end service for her, a coaching program for $7500. She sold out the event and instead of making a couple of thousand dollars a day, she made $45,000. Today she works with someone on a consulting basis. She used to charge $1500 and today she charges $125,000. People might say that sounds crazy. How can she go from $1,500 to $125,000?

Well the truth is, the biggest reason people don't make the money that they want to be making, or are afraid of closing sales, is guilt and shame — around selling, around money, and around themselves. The second reason is fear of not being loved. We're so conditioned to want people to like us. It's such a deep need.

Fill in some of the gaps. What does it look like when a client comes to work with you?

The first thing we do, we spend time looking at what are the thoughts and feelings and perceptions that they have around money. We look at that on a deep level, so we can understand why they're not making the money they want to be making. We look at the set point they have. We all have a set point on what we feel comfortable with.

First of all, I see that there's no lack of money, there's no lack of clients. So I create a brain code activation system. It comes from the premise that we have these connections in our brain that tell us what we're comfortable making and what we should be making. The first process will be to go through a deep training of activating the code in the brain, which is always there, but we're sliding and shifting it until there's no limit to what they believe in their mind they can make.

Step two is to neutralize the guilt and the shame, and the biggest fear that they have around wealth creation, so they can raise their self-worth, stop minimizing themselves, and stop putting clients on pedestals and begin to earn real money.

Step three is putting a productive strategic plan for fast implementation, so we can start making high premium sales, or whatever service they offer. So they can have total certainty about the value they provide.

We create the product, we create the positioning, because you've got to position yourself to stand out in an overcrowded market. That's not going to happen by promising the same result that everybody else does. It's got to be different. And when we do that, they really stand out and they can have high premium clients who love what they have. The only reason for a lack of income is really that were not serving people. Money is really just a means of exchange. The reason we don't have those exchanges is because we have fear. We wouldn't want to admit that because being fearful is not so cool, but that's the truth.

I would love if you could share another example or two of the impact that you've had on your clients through your work.

I'll give you a couple of short ones. I am working with a client in the fitness industry. She used to charge $47 or $97 for products. We looked at her business. She had a list of people she had built over the years, and she heard that the three biggest complaints was that they didn't have time to take care of themselves. They didn't have the money to buy organic food and that kind of stuff. Time was one piece, money was another piece, and they felt they didn't have energy. I designed a coaching program to accelerate their time and money and make sure that they had the energy. We created a program for groups for $7500. You can imagine the growth process for her. In the first 30 days we sold $75,000 worth of coaching for her. The program was at first 12 weeks. After testing this for a while she realized that she could get those same results in 8 weeks. We got her program to be 8 weeks, and instead of charging $7500 she charged $10,000. She had never seen that kind of injection of cash into her bank account that fast before. That came from her understanding her value.

Another example. I had a client who an opportunity to sell into a big corporation and make a seven figure contract. But she didn't really believe, in herself, that she had that value. So what we initiated was a way for her to own her value. I told her, "Listen, these people that you are going to have this meeting with, they have character traits that you believe that you don't have. You put them on a pedestal. You say these are bigwigs, they have this big corporation." So I had her take the five biggest traits that she saw in this person that she was negotiating with. I said, "What do you admire in this person?" And I had her define where she had those exact traits, quantitatively and qualitatively, to the same degree. I had her write down 200 benefits she could bring, the value that she could add to this company.

So when she walked into this meeting, she was not minimizing, or devaluing herself. She put herself on the same level as the CEO, owning her traits. She closed a seven-figure deal. And it happened like that in one conversation. And that's the difference when you own your value.

Satori Mateu is the World's #1 Wealth Mentor. Satori, the #1 Bestselling author of Unshakeable Wealth and creator of Brain Code Activation - an elite performance method to accelerate your success. He most famous for helping thought leaders, experts, and businesses own their value so they can get paid their worth consistently. Satori is of the most sought after and highest paid Wealth and Relationship Mentors on the planet.

YOUR NEXT STEPS

To learn more about Satori and his work, visit his website at www.satorimateu.com, or email him at satori@satorimateu.com. To have him help you to personally reset your money Thermostat and 10X your income absolutely FREE, visit: http://satorimateu.com/wealthaccelerator.

CHAPTER 8:

NADINE HAUPT ON BREAKTHROUGH STRATEGIES FOR ENTREPRENEURS

Interview on CEO Spotlight Radio – September 28, 2016

Tell us a bit about yourself and the evolution of your business.

Over the past 25 years, I've taken an unconventional path to success through multiple industries. Starting as a mechanical engineer in Detroit working for Chrysler, I worked in engine design on the original Dodge Viper V10 engine. It was just phenomenal to have that opportunity! It tapped into my competitive nature and was how I fell in love with professional motor sports.

After a few years at Chrysler I realized I wanted to find a way to get paid to go racing. It took me about two years of focus and determination, but I finally got my foot in the door and joined Honda Performance Development in Southern California as the first female trackside engineer in IndyCar racing.

I spent the next seven years navigating the good ol' boys network in racing. Working for Honda, Mercedes Ilmor, and Ford Cosworth, I tuned race engines while supporting multiple teams and drivers. Tuning engines to get its top performance and how that interplayed with the overall strategy of the competition each weekend really drove my curiosity and my passion.

Eventually I got tired of living out of a suitcase so I wanted to find some way to transition back into the real world. I went to school, got my MBA and made my way back here to Chicago. In 2004, I joined an engineering consulting firm in the far west suburbs as an expert witness for product liability cases in the automotive industry. That was interesting, but I found myself really wanting to do more on the business strategy side of things.

I moved over to Navistar in 2008, which is also known as International Truck and Engine. Besides doing the everyday strategy planning for product development, I took a slight tangent and said, "Well, where do we really need to be in the longer-term future?" That led me to become an expert in alternative fuels, particularly natural gas, for the commercial trucking industry. I was a speaker at industry conferences, and did a lot of training internally with our sales department and our dealer operations.

I thought I had it all figured out until the rug got pulled out from us there at Navistar and we had to switch gears completely. We lost all of the top executives and all of a sudden natural gas and the future of alternative fuels within the company wasn't so important. That's when I realized I could keep reinventing myself. I truly believed that there are no limits, only choices.

One of the things that I knew for many years was my desire to be my own boss and to serve clients in a way that was unique to me to help them create breakthrough results. In 2014, I took the leap from Corporate America. I started my own business to help entrepreneurs use a strategic, structured and authentic approach to business development and client attraction.

So you've been able to apply skills acquired in the automotive industry to helping entrepreneurs?

When I looked back through the 20 years prior to starting my own business, there were two common threads. One was the strategic perspective: I was always building strategies, whether it was in racing or taking an approach to a legal case as an expert witness, or developing the vision to deliver alternative fueled vehicles for commercial trucking. I knew I could bring that to my clients, help them leverage their own knowledge and expertise.

The other thread was speaking, whether it was being interviewed multiple times on ESPN and on magazine-type shows such as Inside Cart, or talking at industry conferences. I was a spokesperson for Navistar, so whenever we had big launches I helped with press releases and press conferences, and walked the analysts from Wall Street through the new product. I had a knack for speaking and getting results. That seemed like another way I could help clients market themselves.

What do your clients look like?

My ideal clients are mission-driven entrepreneurs. They're folks that have a tremendous amount of expertise and talent and want to make a difference in the world. But they're struggling to find the right clients and to attract the right people. They're not making the sales they need to really take that vision to bigger and greater heights. They struggle because they're scattered with their approach. I love to work with them to get focused on their compelling offer and their signature, unique process. Once we have a foundation of that model then there are multiple streams of income we can create by replicating what they already know.

My clients are solopreneurs and companies with maybe less than ten people that are nimble and willing to make small changes to achieve big breakthroughs. My premier program, which I work with one-on-one clients and am about to offer as a group program, is called the Speak More, Sell More Blueprint.

When I made the transition into entrepreneurship, I knew that speaking was going to be the most effective and efficient way for me to market myself and my new business. I approached it with the same strategy I'd used in the corporate world. I was giving away a lot of great content. I was educating and teaching, and the audiences found it great, which was awesome, but they'd walk right out the door. I realized I needed to do something different if I was going to sell my own services and products.

That's what founded this process, the 5 Ps that make up the Speak More, Sell More Blueprint, which not only gives great value, but also allows you to create that flow of clients, who are self-selecting and say, "Hey, I need to do more work with you."

Some clients that come to me are very creative and have big visions for how they want to make an impact on the world. The problem has been they don't have the structure in place to be able to capitalize on that vision. Sometimes we have to narrow the focus, get one piece together first - whether that's a workshop, a VIP day, a high-ticket coaching package or a group program. Whatever fits the needs of their ideal client, that's what we focus on. Then we can start looking at how to leverage that and serve more and more people and continue to build the business.

What are your clients saying after they come out of this process?

The biggest response I get from clients is relief and excitement. I say relief because they're coming to me stressed out. They've got umpteen balls that they're tossing up in the air and they just can't keep it all straight. When we get some clarity, it gives them permission to let go of other things and not feel like they have to do everything all at once.

I had a great conversation with a client recently who had the whole list of things that she wanted to do. She wanted to launch a YouTube channel show. She wanted to write a book. She wanted to do more keynote speaking. But she could see that there are only so many hours in the day and days in the year. We looked at what made the most sense for her and then let the other things go, pushed them further back – not completely off the table, but just to say, "Let's focus on these things first." That's where the excitement comes in, because now they're like, "Okay, I know what I have to do."

What's different in your life? How are you different today as a result of this journey?

I look now at my transition from corporate into entrepreneurship and realize there were some things that I knew and there were a lot of things that I didn't know. In my corporate world I had a network of people that I could talk to and bounce things off of and strategize with, but when I stepped out on my own I realized that I was out there by myself. I had to seek the community of other like-minded individuals, people that were on that same journey of entrepreneurship because they could truly understand the challenges and the things that were coming up for me.

That's the support that I needed. And that's what I'm trying to do for my clients. Some of them have been working a side hustle for a while and they want to finally make the transition and do that full-time. Others have just been struggling. They've got the great idea but they haven't put it together. Having that smaller community of strong support is what I feel I bring to the table and what a lot of my clients really enjoy.

I encourage my clients to create an environment of curiosity. The beautiful thing that we have here in this country is the opportunities. There truly is an opportunity to be limitless in what you want to do and achieve. By being curious, you keep yourself open to any and all opportunities that might present themselves that perhaps you maybe never even saw coming.

Nadine Haupt – "The Breakthrough Strategist" – works with motivated and results-driven leaders and entrepreneurs who are eager to break through barriers and accelerate their impact and income substantially using a strategic, structured, and authentic approach to client attraction and business development.

If you are looking for a proven professional who can guide you to address what is standing in your way of success, show you how to create endless opportunities for growth, and lead you on your own unique path, you are in the right place.

Since 1994, Nadine blazed a successful trail from pit lane to the corporate boardroom by taking the road not traveled – including becoming the first female trackside engineer in IndyCar Racing. She has navigated the twists and turns of start-ups, niche businesses, consulting firms, multi-national corporations and entrepreneurship to take an unconventional path to success in multiple male-dominated industries.

Nadine's core philosophy - "There are no limits, only choices" – inspires and guides clients worldwide to fuel their passion to greatness and build a business and life they love. Nadine's clients are drawn to her passion, authenticity, professionalism, and down-to-earth style. Her no-nonsense approach challenges clients, while her compassion and support encourages them to make bold moves.

Her first book, Fall in Love with Monday Mornings: A Career Woman's Guide to Increasing Impact, Influence, and Income, was released in June 2015.

YOUR NEXT STEPS

Visit http://nadinehaupt.com/free-gift-from-nadine/ to download your FREE Chapter of Nadine's book.

To learn more, visit NadineHaupt.com, visit www.linkedin.com/in/nrhaupt/ to connect with Nadine on LinkedIn, www.facebook.com/NadineTheBreakthroughStrategist/ on Facebook, and @BkthrStrategist on Twitter.

CHAPTER 9:

DR. SARAH REIFF-HEKKING ON MANAGING YOUR TIME

**Interview on CEO Spotlight Radio –
November 2, 2016**

*Share with us how you got interested in
helping people around procrastination and
being overwhelmed?*

Well, I tell you, Howard, I come to it
very honestly. I started my career as a
clinical psychologist. My struggle with
procrastination really showed up in
graduate school. I would just get so
overwhelmed with the amount of things that I needed to do that
I would either avoid them, or feel kind of frozen and have a hard
time moving forward.

One of my worst examples happened when I was a research
assistant on this amazing study I was so excited to be a part of.
My job was to go into the hospital and interview people that had
recently had heart attacks. I'd have them fill out some questions,
then go to the medical chart, get some more information, then go
back to my apartment and fill out yet more paperwork, and send
it back to the research hospital in order to get paid. And what
would happen is that I would do most of the work, but I
wouldn't do those last few steps that allowed me to get paid. So I

literally had this pile of paper that was money. But I wasn't able to convert it into money because it was still sitting on my desk.

So I want people to know that when you're struggling with procrastination and overwhelm, I've been there. I understand how it feels to have that stack of money on your desk that you're not able to make real in your life. So in graduate school it got really clear to me that I needed to work through that, otherwise it was going to cause long term problems for me. So I started to figure out how to break things down into smaller chunks and create systems. And through the last 10 years in my coaching practice, I've developed systems that work for me and my clients that struggle with these issues.

Why are some individuals affected while others just get things done? Is this upbringing? Is it mentoring? How does that happen?

I think that most people, most of us in the United States, struggle with time management issues at this point. Because we are so inundated by incoming information with our electronics. I think most people feel like "There's something wrong with me. Why can't I do this right? Why can't I figure this out in the way other people have figured it out?" There's really two things that come up for me when I talk to people about this. The first one is, we're all wired a little bit differently. We're born with strengths and weaknesses in terms of how we think about planning, how we're able to notice that time is passing, and how we're able to implement those kinds of skills in our environment.

On top of that, we have different learning histories. So that's the psychological fancy-shmancy way of saying some of us are taught these skills or learn these skills more readily in either our school environment or our home environment. And then others of us haven't had this kind of training or mentoring that allows us to manage all the incoming information, all the things that need to get done, to prioritize them, plan them, and then make them happen in our life.

And for the individuals where this is a big issue, what's the impact?

What I find is that procrastination and overwhelm cause problems for people because they start to not trust themselves anymore. You get stuck in this negative spiral where you procrastinate, or you avoid, or you freeze. We all have something – it's a different flavor for each one of us, so you need to get clear about what that is. But that emotion catches us and we procrastinate or we avoid, then we feel worse, and then we procrastinate, we avoid, and we keep feeling worse. So it digs us into that hole of negative emotion that is the opposite of what we need to be able to be productive.

How do issues of time management show up?

I see four different areas. Some people have a hard time feeling in control and noticing that time is passing. Some people experience time as right now, or sometime in the future. And if that's you, you can learn skills to help you manage that, so that time doesn't just evaporate or fly by. I also see people have problems with planning –what's a to-do list, what's a calendar system that works for you, that you know you can rely on. And then I also see problems in terms of goal setting and priorities.

So what I see with leaders a lot is there's long-term goals and there's what has to happen right now. And sometimes we don't set up the glue between where we want to go and where we are in this moment. And that's really a problem with setting priorities and learning skills so that you can steer your day, your week, your month, your year, to end up where you want to. And then there's also that emotional piece of procrastination and overwhelm that we need to get a handle on.

What all of these areas add up to is difficulty reaching that next level in our life that we crave. And I see so often with leaders, that they're so busy getting all of the nuts and bolts done, that they don't have the time or the bandwidth to think about what is it that they want to create? Where do they want to go?

Can you share an example of the impact it's had, after you've worked with a client?

Absolutely. I'm thinking of a leader I'm working with right now, a CEO of his own company. It's a marketing agency. He's been in my Time Matters bootcamp, which is a group program that I run. What happens when people come into that program, or come into private work with me is that they come in feeling really overwhelmed by the day to day tasks that are showing up for them. There's not enough time to get stuff done. So there's this craziness about enrolling in a program, or working with somebody that takes up more time to help them get more done.

But as they learn skills and put in place some of the systems that I teach, their planning horizon goes from right now and the next 24 hours, to out a week. Then out even a month. So they're able to relax, know that the most important things are going to get handled, and create that space for the bigger picture thinking, the bigger picture dreaming that they've been craving.

So for instance, just this past week, a CEO of his own marketing company said to me, wow, so now I know the basic stuff of running my company is handled, I don't have to worry about that. I have the space to think about what is the really impactful work I want to do. I can take myself and my people to that next level. And he also says things like: I'm able to have more fun. I exercise more. I enjoy the day more. And I know I'm doing the most important work that only I can do in the world.

The other side effect is people often end up making more money, because they're really clear about what are the most important revenue generating activities for them and their team.

So it sounds like your clients see a return on investment in the form of tangible results.

Yes. Something I really want to share with you, Howard, and your audience. I think this is really going to be transformational for them. Let's just say for easy math that I can help you be more productive on something that's really important for an hour a day. Over a year, that's 365 hours. That ends up being over nine 40-hour work weeks. What is the value to you, of nine 40-hour work weeks? For most of us it's huge, it's thousands of dollars.

Can you share a little bit more about your system. What are the steps you take them through?

So I have a larger framework that I work with, and within that I share these five steps to bust your procrastination and overwhelm that are really life-altering for many people. The first step is to recognize what's overwhelming you. Let's say there's a huge fire-breathing dragon that lives outside your village. He's five stories tall, he breathes fire and he has a tail as big as your house. So he's not a little bitty dragon. He's huge, and he can do a lot of damage. If that was your life, you would first want to know where that dragon lived. So the first thing in terms of busting through procrastination and overwhelm is recognize what's overwhelming you, or what I like to call *find the beast.*

So you want to start to notice where that negative emotion related to procrastination or overwhelm shows up for you. And that's going to give you a lot of great information. For instance, you might notice that there's something on your to-do list that you keep copying over from week to week. Ask yourself, am I procrastinating or avoiding that thing, and why? And that's going to give you a hint about what's getting in the way.

The second step is to calm the inner fear discussion. And that's *taming the dragon.* So we all have negative stuff that goes through our head. You want to get a handle on what that is. It usually sounds like, I can't do this, I have too much to do, I'm not good enough. You want to acknowledge what that negative fear discussion is and create a positive discussion that's consistent with productivity. So that's the mindset piece in the system.

The next step is really an environmental piece. You want to set up your routine and your environment to support productivity. What I like to call *engineering your containment system*. And it really is like setting up a perimeter around your village so the dragon's not going to come in. I want you to set up your daily and weekly routines, and your physical environment to keep procrastination at bay.

And then step four is really *get support*, because if you're struggling with procrastination or overwhelm, you need some help with it. You're too close to it to really break out of it on your own. Success never happens alone. No matter who you think is successful on their own, if you peel back the curtain you know that there's a great support team behind the curtain.

The last step is really *keep restarting* until you're where you need to be. So finishing a big task, keep starting it, keep starting it, keep starting it until it's finished.

Dr. Sarah Reiff-Hekking is the founder of True Focus Coaching Inc., a speaker, coach, and Psychologist with 20 years of experience helping people create the lives they crave. She is passionate about helping smart people that have a hard time managing their time and their tasks, figure out a way that works for them. She believes that you have to find the time management system that works for you, that solutions are found by paying attention to the present moment, and that just like Michelangelo had to chip away at the stone to find the statue, we have to get rid of all the extra stuff that isn't the core of your life.

YOUR NEXT STEPS

To learn more about Dr. Reiff-Hekking and her work, visit her website at www.TrueFocusCoaching.com. Be sure to take the True Focus Quiz to learn more about your Time Management Skills and opt-in to the True Focus Coaching Email Newsletter.

CHAPTER 10:

STACEY CANFIELD ON CREATING COMPELLING FIRST IMPRESSIONS

Interview on Your Success Path Live – December 14, 2016

Tell us something about your background.

My path started 30 years ago. I was 18 years old, in high school, and I went to a career day where there was a professional photographer, and I just went "wow, I can really be creative and have a career," so I went up after the presentation and I complimented him and his wife. They both looked at each other and they looked at me and said, "do you want a job?" And I got hired on the spot. Although I was doing reception work, and I was answering phones, and I was carding negatives (which is a term no one uses anymore because everything's digital) it really gave me my start.

It also showed me how a mom-and-pop shop can run. Fast forward 30 years, my husband and I still run a very successful studio, so it's just funny how you're influenced at an early age. I started at 18. I got the Master Craftsman degree for my industry at 28. And I focused on portraiture because I really love people. I love the individual expression and I love relationships. So maybe it's between a mother and child, or a husband and wife – I love capturing those kind of relationships. True joy, true love, that's what I love capturing, and that's why I love focusing on heart-centered entrepreneurs who have a message that they need to get out into the world. I am honored to be charged with capturing that so they can make that great first impression online.

Is it more important for an entrepreneur to establish a brand now than it used to be?

Absolutely. Before, if you were an executive in a company, you might get a professional photo taken maybe once every five years. And it would hang as an eight by ten in a frame in the middle of the lobby, or in the boardroom, or somewhere prominent in the company. No longer does that work. We have LinkedIn, where people see you on a daily basis. We have company websites, your reach is so much larger. So what's interesting about how photography has morphed over the years is that yes, there is a place for the formal portrait, which I can create, but there's also a place for the more casual, authentic lifestyle photo as well, where it shows people in their element, and how they interact with people.

There's even room for the selfie. So a selfie isn't great for a professional photo on your LinkedIn profile, but it does have a place in your blog or on social media. If you are doing something great, you've just won an award, you're offstage and grabbing a selfie or you have a friend take a picture of you with the award you just won, those are great things to put on social media. It's quick, it's genuine, it's authentic, it's in the moment, and people want to see that. But when you're trying to represent yourself and make that great first impression, you have to be a little strategic about it. So that's what I do when I work more closely with my clients – we sit down and have a strategic plan of what your image is, and how you want it to get out into the world.

Is this something your clients are comfortable with?

Honestly I think for a lot of executives and entrepreneurs, this is the last thing they want to think about. They'd probably rather go get their teeth drilled in a dentist's chair than be photographed. A lot of my clients have a little bit of trepidation before they come see me. They don't know if it's going to hurt. They don't know if emotionally they're prepared for it.

Being photographed can be very emotional, so what I pride myself on is I have a wonderful system that really walks people through the process to completely prepare them to step into the camera room. It's my Face of Your Brand formula, and it goes through all the emotional preparation, the physical preparation. I even get down to what colors look best on you to wear in the camera room. That kind of preparation allows people to feel their best so their true essence can come forward and shine through.

We wear our body like we wear clothes, and there are tips and tricks that I've learned over the years that minimize trouble areas. There are angles that can enhance positive features and diminish things that we don't want to bring out. But I think what's most important is embody your body. Own it. Oprah is at her best when she lives her authentic self. Her ratings weren't as big when she was a stick figure. She is a beautiful role model of embodying her body, and just finding out what works best for her, what colors work best for her. She lives the joy that she wants to bring to the world, and she focuses on the message and the purpose of her being in the world, and that's what shines through. And those are the little mental games that I get to play with you in the camera room is – let's focus on your purpose. Once you focus on your purpose, and your message, and what you really want to convey, the truth is going to come forward in your photo, and that's going to be the most attractive quality.

I have the five must-have photos that everyone needs if you're a speaker and you want to get online. So, I walk people through those five must-haves and we shoot for those. For instance, you really need to have a great speaker photo that

Your Path to Business Success

shows you as you would be animated on stage. So if you're a demure TED Talk speaker, we're going to photograph you in the energy of giving that speech. If you're vivacious and active on stage, we're going to capture that, because we need to show those event hosts what you're going to look like on their stage. We also need to make sure you have a good guest photo, to show your happiest, friendliest smile. Then we have three others as well.

What kind of feedback do you get?

The most common is: "Stacey, you really get me," like they're being seen for the first time. I think everybody has a certain way they imagine themselves. If they could close their eyes, they imagine themselves this way. But maybe it's not quite reflected in the mirror the way they want it to. So we try to tap into that feeling that they want to embody, and bring that forward.

Bottom line is the relationship that I have with them. It's like these people are with me at a cocktail party, and there's some great music playing behind, and we're just having a great time. I'm telling you, a smile is everything. There's only one exception, and that would be an author photo, where if you have a really heavy topic you won't want to be smiling. But for everything else it's that winning smile that attracts people. If you're talking about something you love, and you're in a workshop, your enthusiasm is what's going to show up, and that's the enthusiasm that I would capture live.

How do you begin that process?

The first step with my clients is I put them through a professional photo audit, and we look at what they've been working with previously. We're going to look at their LinkedIn profile photo, their current website, their speaker photo, all that, and we're going to assess it. What's working? Where is there room for improvement?

Then we go into a photo strategy session. We assess what your needs are. You need a new photo for your home page web banner. You need a new photo for your sales page opt-in. You need a new profile photo for Facebook and LinkedIn. Then we decide what colors work best for your speaker photo, your product photo, your profile photo. I help you with your photo color code that you can take with you shopping. That's really helpful. The next step is just getting you in the camera room.

I have this event that I do a couple times a year. It's called a BrandStorm retreat, and it's special because I only allow three people to participate at a time. So it's very exclusive, invitation only. People hear about it through the grapevine. I invite three special entrepreneurs to go through my Face of Your Brand system and then they come to San Diego for two days. We spend a full day in my home. First they go through my process called the Dream Brand Assessment, where I assess their business and come up with a vision for their brand, so that they can reinvent themselves. The second day we take tons of pictures.

When you photograph someone, it's very intimate, especially in post-production when you're pouring through all of the images, retouching them, and choosing photos – it's a very intimate time. So I really get to know these women deeply, and they're happy, and they're laughing, and they're feeling their best.

So what's next for you?

My next step is to create a virtual boot camp where I can enroll 20, 30, 40 people in my system at a time. That will launch early 2017. It's going to give people an opportunity to learn my system and get group coaching. You'll be able to hear my voice once a week on the phone and ask questions, and it'll walk you through my five step process, which prepares you very well to step up and be photographed anywhere, by any photographer.

Stacey Canfield is an acclaimed photographer, author and personal branding expert, supports women entrepreneurs to become the face of their brand. With over 30 years of photography experience, as well as a former model, she brings both an eye for detail and a heart-centered focus to transforming the image, confidence and brand of her clientele. So much more than just great pictures, Stacey incorporates personalized elements of color, style, posture and personality to create photos that truly capture and communicate each client's unique individuality to the world. In today's online world, your image is your brand. Stacey makes sure the true you shines through.

Stacey has achieved the photography industry's highest degree - Master Craftsmen and has been a partner in Visual Photography, a studio located in North County San Diego since 1994. Her true gift is uncovering and expressing each client's authentic self on film with her fun and nurturing portrait sessions. She offers both individual and group programs that will transform your brand, your business, your confidence and your life. Stacey's ultimate gift is empowering entrepreneurs to be confident and ready to be the face of their brand.

YOUR NEXT STEPS

To learn more about Stacey's work, and discover her Signature Programs, visit her website at www.myimageartist.com. And make sure to request a Professional Photo Audit.

Visit www.linkedin.com/in/staceygreencanfield/ to connect with Stacey on LinkedIn, www.facebook.com/MyImageArtist/ to connect on Facebook, and @MyImageArtist on Twitter.

CHAPTER 11:

KRISTEN NOLAN ON HEALTHY HABITS FOR BUSY PROFESSIONALS

Interview on CEO Spotlight Radio – December 20, 2016

Share a bit about yourself and the work you're doing.

I am a health and metabolism expert for busy professionals. I help to bring your health and your energy to your attention so that you can perform better in business and in life. The reason that I'm so passionate about this is because about ten years ago I had built up a very successful business. I had a boot camp and then I opened up my own fitness studio in San Francisco. With those two locations, I was doing well getting clients in, but my health started taking a nosedive. For a fitness professional, this was pretty unacceptable.

When did you being to realize something was wrong?

It started out with some minor digestive discomforts, and I just chose to ignore them. I was like, "I'm too busy to deal with this right now. I have clients to see. I have marketing campaigns to run, so I'm just going to keep pushing forward and doing the best that I can." When you're overly stressed your ability to digest and break down food is highly compromised. In fact, if you're in this realm for a long period of time your digestive function can decrease its efficiency by up to 50%. That's what was happening to me. I started feeling sick after eating grilled chicken and salad. I mean, what the heck? Like even after eating healthy foods, I was not feeling well. My energy just took a real nosedive because I wasn't digesting food and assimilating nutrients. I didn't know that at the time, but now I know that's what happened. I started developing what I call this little stress belly. That's when you feel like you're eating the right things, you're working out, but nothing is coming off you weight-wise.

I started not sleeping through the night, and this is because when your body is overly stressed it can't tell the difference between you're being chased by a bear and might die or you're just having a crazy day at work. I was getting really moody. I found myself fighting to put on a show, acting like I had it all together when every single day on the inside I felt like I was falling apart. It was very painful for me for a while. My digestion wasn't good, my energy was below zero. I was tired all the time. It was like these things just built on top of each other until I was so uncomfortable and so beyond exhausted and unmotivated that I knew I needed to get help. I had to shut down one of my fitness locations because I couldn't handle the toll it was taking on my body. I was about $30,000 in debt.

So I hired a metabolism coach, and the information she had for me saved my life – and I truly believe that. I was really on the edge there for a while. There was a point when I was hospitalized with terrible gall bladder pain that I couldn't figure out how to get rid of. It was not good. So I learned different types of nutrition strategies to keep my energy up, I learned movement strategies to use when I was stressed out, which had nothing to do with working my body really, really hard, and I ended up healing myself from the inside out.

I finally had the energy again to run my business effectively. I got myself out of debt and I made six figures the next year. It really is a testament to what happens when you start prioritizing your body and your health. That experience has driven me to want to help as many high performing men and women to set a solid foundation for themselves health-wise, so they can have the confidence to be on stage, so they can have the energy to close sales, and so they have the stamina to create the difference that they really want to make in their business.

How do you help leaders and entrepreneurs take better care of themselves physically?

I love working with high performers and Type A personalities, and because they are so driven in their business and they're used to investing in their business, taking a step back and prioritizing their health is quite a new experience for them. I found that the best way for me to serve my clients and work with them effectively is through a boutique concierge-like service. I see my clients six times a month over Skype, which means that we're seeing each other once or twice a week. I'm able to really hold their hand through the process, and help them to prioritize their bodies, which is something that left to their own devices they probably would not do.

For example, I was working with an entrepreneur, and when we were first on the phone, she was confiding in me that it had gotten so bad that she didn't recognize herself in the mirror anymore, her energy was so low. She told me that because she had a bunch of brain fog and she just wasn't feeling motivated that she was finding it really hard to be productive in her business. Well, with her we really had to hold her hand through the process and have her actually schedule in time to take care of herself – 45-minute sessions with me, and then scheduling time for her to do things that she loved, like taking a walk, getting grounded again.

After learning how to prioritize yourself, there are really three areas that we work with. There's getting your metabolism on point by showing you how to energize your body with food combinations. There's getting your movements on point by showing you different movements that are light and easy on the body and will help you activate all your muscles so you can feel toned and strong. Then there's finding ways to stay relaxed and happy, because the stress is always going to be there.

Step by step we took this client through this process, and she felt like a million bucks afterwards, super energized. She was able to focus for the whole day and not just part of the day. She didn't get that mid-afternoon crash anymore. And she ended up making $5000 more a month in her business because she was able to see clients all day.

It's really interesting how taking a step back and refocusing on yourself can help you spring forward into the next level of success. I think it's just having somebody there to hold you accountable and show you that it's okay to do that because you're so not used to that being okay.

With a new client, how do you begin working?

I have a few different ways that clients will work with me, but ultimately we always use what I call my Fit For Success Formula. The very first step in the formula is to define your personal body balance code. What that means is we look at what is working for you, or what you love to do movement-wise, the food combinations that you love to eat, and what keeps you relaxed and happy. Being relaxed and happy is so important because when you're body's super stressed you hold onto extra weight, and it really doesn't matter what else you do.

Once we're figured out their personal movement, food, and mood code, that becomes their baseline for success. They get a personalized checklist so they know exactly what steps to do every day, and then we take it from there. They've got a bunch of supportive tools, meal plans, grocery lists, all that fun stuff, and this virtual metabolism makeover system I have. But then on top of that we are seeing each other six times a month while they integrate their body balance code. It always takes a while to integrate this, because typically the client is flying in a million different directions. So we work on it piece by piece so their body ends up feeling lighter. They have more fun with the process, it doesn't become this torturous thing where they're always like blaming themselves for not doing a million things at once, and they actually enjoy it. I love seeing my clients regularly because we laugh together, they're able to really get my support, I share with them, they share with me. It's just amazing because I'm able to hold their hand through the entire process.

What I've found is that most of the people that work really well with me have already gotten to a point where they've built their business up, they're pretty successful, but then they really have this drive to take it to the next level. They want to get out there, they want to speak on stages, they want to do videos. They don't want to feel self-conscious, they want to really own their message. I've found that when they have this doubt monster in the back of their head, driving them down and killing their confidence, because maybe they don't feel as fit or energized as they want to feel, then this can really impact their performance.

Share some of your success stories.

I'll give you an example. I had a client who wanted to do a launch in 90 days, but she was at a point where everything she chose to eat for lunch would make her blood sugar crash. She couldn't figure out why, because the foods she was eating were "healthy," so she was really frustrated. She was like, "You know what? I'm losing so many hours of productivity, and this is really killing my business. I can't see clients after lunch. I can't go to networking events." I think she was actually making the success connection in her head before she and I spoke on the phone.

We got her started on a program and first we looked at what her body balance code was for her metabolism. We chose three easy meal combinations that she could eat for lunch that made her feel more energized. Once she was no longer crashing at the 3:00 p.m. slot, she could see more clients and she could prep her body to have a successful launch. That launch period for entrepreneurs is so taxing. You need to be in good physical shape. So many entrepreneurs get sick at that time, or develop what I call launch belly, or just exhaust themselves.

So we set her up for success. Three months later she has her launch. She generates $30,000 in sales. She does this amazing talk from the stage, adds 500 people to her list, she's over the moon. Having your energy doesn't sound like it's that big of a deal, but it really does matter. When you're showing up consistently in this way, your prospects, your ideal clients are going to see that. You're going to magnetize them. It's like you're pulling them to you because they're just like, "Wow, I want to be her." But for them to want to be you, you have to show up authentically. The way you present yourself truly does matter. When you look like a stress case, people see that, they lose their trust in you.

Where do you see yourself taking this in the next couple of years?

Looking ahead, I see myself in the next couple years speaking on way more stages, speaking virtually, spreading the message that your body is all you have when it comes to being successful in your business and staying present in your personal life. I want to travel more and I want to continue my boutique-style business seeing clients over Skype. I'm also starting a Fit For Success podcast, so we'll see where that takes us. But I have trouble planning five or ten years out. I change with the times and do what I love always, because that's what keeps what I do so important to me, which radiates to the world.

Kristen Nolan, the High Performance Health Mentor, is a fitness & metabolism expert who helps busy, professional women and men learn to take back control of their bodies so they feel energized, physically fit, and confident in business and life!

She is a best-selling author, international speaker and has helped thousands of women and men nationwide with simple techniques to naturally increase metabolism and energy. Kristen has developed several programs, including her "Metabolism Makeover Academy," "Fit for a Stage" and "Fit for Success" to teach career focused women and men how to overcome food cravings, feel lean, regain their youthful vitality, and make the process fun and rewarding so they stay committed to the process and happily maintain their results for life!

YOUR NEXT STEPS

To learn more about Kristen's work, visit her at kristennolan.com, and link to her free gift at kristennolan.com/get-started/.

Connect with Kristen on LinkedIn at www.linkedin.com/in/healthexpertkristennolan, follow her on Facebook at www.facebook.com/ILuvMyBodyFitness/, and on Twitter at @Kristenolan.

Chapter 12:

Ashley Ryan & Bruce Spurr on Leading While Being a Boss

Interview on
Your Success
Path Live –
January 25, 2017

Ashley: There's a lot of great information out there online and there's a lot of ridiculous information. Having a brick and mortar business is completely different from having an online business. We wanted to launch a show where we would bust some myths and just be real with people about what's working and what's not working and what to do to make it in business. It drives us both crazy when we see these people touting things that just aren't true.

I remember going to a T. Harv Eker event and he said, "If I could give you one piece of advice, it would be to focus on one thing and do it well, and do it over again." I didn't take that advice. Ten years later, my successes have come from rinsing and repeating, having a really narrow focus. It's the distractions that throw us off.

Bruce: We both have a long track record of successes and failures. Over the last dozen years, we've seen each other rise and fall, rise and fall.

Ashley: Through thick and through thin.

Bruce: A lot of people think entrepreneurs start businesses on their own. But going to programs, going to conferences, there's nothing better than learning from the guy sitting next to you who's going through the same struggles, trying to achieve the same goals that you are. The camaraderie and support you can build for each other is phenomenal.

Ashley: I just want to add that, in order to grow and move beyond, you have to have a team. I thought when I started out that I could just hand things over, delegate everything. I can work minimally these days, but I'm still involved. I'm still leading. Your team can add tons of value (beyond the work they do). The days that I feel down, my team's there. Just because I'm the boss doesn't mean they don't lift me up. And the same for them. They're having a rough day and I'm there.

Bruce: People start with the idea that being a leader means being a boss and having people that you manage. But it's not just about assigning tasks. Mostly you inspire them to do great work, tell them what the framework is that you are trying to establish, where you want to go, how you want to get there, the values you'd like to embody as you move down that path. If you can set those as bumpers, then people just kind of bounce back and forth between them as you guys work together to achieve something.

That changes as you grow. With one person, you're working in a partnership. With two or three, it is like a small circle. There's more complexity because of more relationships. At five and six, all of a sudden you have to take on more of a facilitation role and allow the ideas to generate from the group. At 10, all of a sudden you can't even take on the facilitation role because it's just too big. You start putting middle managers in play and a bunch of other things. You can't take care of everybody. The thing that you do as a leader changes completely. You're removing yourself more and more from the day-to-day grind and idea generation. I think that's the biggest challenge that people have in leadership.

Ashley: Saying to someone, "I'll give it to you, I'll hand it over."

Bruce: It's nerve-racking. The first time it happened to me in 2001. I remember it like it was yesterday. Half of me was elated and the other half of me was like, "Oh my god, I mean if you don't do a good job on this, that's my reputation." The anxiety – it was like a huge high and a huge low at the exact same time. It ended up working out, but it doesn't always. That's really when leadership comes in. What do you do when it doesn't work out?

Ashley: The ability to work through things. It's like any relationship. The worst thing is to be a dictator. It isn't very practical. It builds resentment. But when you are more of a fair boss and it's more of a collaborative effort, you still have to work through stuff.

I have a good example of this. A team member was going through some emotional stuff and her work was unreliable and inconsistent. I really like her. The team really likes her. But things were not getting done. The old Ashley might have just totally axed her. In some cases you need to do that, you need to let someone go. But her attitude and her energy, and her wanting to be there made a difference. If you are doing unreliable work and your heart's not really in it, you can tell. This woman wanted to be there and she wanted to work through it. I had to invest in some mindset work and some other things outside of work for her to do, to help her overcome some of her issues. And now it's totally fine. She is one of our top performers.

Bruce: It's your evolution as a leader. You start off with the ability to just take on any task and crush it. Then you step up to working with other people. Then you trust them to take on tasks. When it doesn't work out, that's the fourth level – learning how to deal with that. It comes with a lot patience and experience. I've been around people who have been in leadership roles for 20, 30 years and still haven't gotten to that level. They're at level two, just dictating roles and then using carrot-and-stick models of behavior modification. I'll fire you if you don't figure it out. Or I'll give you a raise, or a promotion, or whatever if you do.

We all know, if we look at the history of behavior science starting with Maslow in the 60s, that carrot-and-stick only hits the first two levels of motivation. To get up to third, fourth, fifth, we're talking about building self-confidence, connection, and then self-actualization. The only way you can do that with people is if you work with them in a more collaborative, facilitative way – doing what Ashley did. First of all, having the wisdom to understand that the person is worth investing in, and second of all, what would it take to get that person moving.

Ashley: If I fired her and had to look for someone else and invest in them, it would still be an effort. The question is, should I take that effort and would it pay off? I took the chance to keep her on and it worked out. But it doesn't necessarily. You have to communicate with a certain consistency.

Bruce: Because here's the thing, the half-life of information is about six weeks. We are going to remember half of this show in six weeks. In another 12 weeks we'll remember about 10% of it. Then a year up the road, we'll just remember that we were on Howard's show. We had a good time. We'll remember one or two stories or details if something really triggers a memory.

If you think about what you tell employees – here's where we want to go, here's how we want to get there – that needs to be reiterated to your team every six weeks at minimum. After six weeks, people will remember half of what you told them. They'll remember that, oh yeah, we deal with problems on our own before asking for help, or we raise our hands if we are struggling so we don't fall too far behind the eight ball. Whatever the mindset of your organization, if you don't consistently communicate that with people, they're never going to remember. They are just going to fill in the blanks with their own values and belief systems, and we know how chaotic that can become.

Ashley: Yes, being a leader is all about repetition.

Bruce: Here's the difference between a level two versus a level four leadership style. At level two you're using results as a motivator. You're telling people, you did that wrong, you did this right, you can go out for lunch, you can't, whatever. At level four, results are just a meter for how I'm doing as a leader, setting those boundaries and explaining what we need to accomplish as a team. If somebody is struggling emotionally, whether outside of work or in work, that's a part of the leadership role too.

It used to be, in the 80s and 90s, people thought that when you walk into the work place you're in work mode and when you go home you're in family mode. Well, we're human beings. Our brains don't compartmentalize like that. Trying to create those barriers actually limits our ability to tap into the full potential of our employees.

Ashley: If you can't be vulnerable people won't stick to you. I am not saying you spill your whole life. But I do share personal things with my team within a certain range. Like, "okay yeah I'm dating someone new" or "I bought a new piece of art" versus "last night's sex was wild" or "I got in a rage and destroyed something." There's a line.

Bruce: I use the analogy of a leader being like a rock, which is the classical view – dependable with all the answers, the one everyone clings to. Once in a while you have to be the rock. You have to be still, and allow other people to be the water that flows around. Especially in crisis mode. Any time you're in a crisis situation, people need that stoicism, that dependability, that rock solidness in your leadership. That should be the leadership trait that manifests during those times. But for the rest of the time, for the day-to-day activity, you have to be like water. You've got to flow, carry people along, help them move down the current. If they're stuck, help them get unstuck. Break them down if they are feeling too rigid in their thinking, be adaptable and agile.

I worked with the military here in Canada for a bit. For decades they've had a philosophy of mission first, team second, individual last. You sacrifice anything to get the mission done first – that's the number one priority – whether it's family, yourself, your health, your welfare, whatever it is. What they found in exploration, especially in the most elite teams, is that if you put the individual needs first, and then the team, and then the mission last, you get exponentially better results. On an individual basis, people feel like they get cared about, and get supported and picked up. It changes the mentality, not just of the individual, but of the entire mechanism. The whole organization comes together to support the individual. If everybody gets supported like that, it lifts up everything else. The mission itself is almost superfluous, it's basically guaranteed that it's going to happen.

It's a mentality that takes quite a while to develop, especially in an organization of that size. What they've found is that when people are not on mission, not in theater, when they're at their headquarters or on their base, if they still get regimented, like they do when they're in combat, they don't respond the same way. You don't get the same level of discipline and care, and you get a lot of PTSD. You get a lot of depression and mental illnesses that then impact the physical output of performance. On the base, they're learning how to manage people in a more collaborative, more engaging way. They're being the water. Then in combat they can be the rocks. Strangely, the more freedom you give people the more disciplined they get.

Ashley: I love that. It's awesome.

Bruce: Being an entrepreneur means overcoming those hurdles. You're going to feel tired. You're going to feel let down constantly. It's not all roses and walks in parks. I take a lot of walks in parks these days. But it's been 16 years of 100-hour work weeks to get to that point. I started my first dot.com in the dot-com bubble and in 2000 that thing imploded. I had to go get a corporate job just to make ends meet. I was literally taking my salary and investing it straight into the business. I used to go to work at 8:30, come home at 5:00, put my bag down and work until 2:00am.

Ashley: I remember those days.

Bruce: And like 16 hours every Saturday and Sunday. For a year and a half, I kept that going. You need to be able to do that to give you the sense of whether or not you can put up with the highs and the lows of being an entrepreneur. It really is a litmus test.

Ashley: And you need to have a cushion. Because the worst thing is building a business when you're broke and stressed and desperate. So you need some sort of stability in order to make that transition. Sometimes you just have to take the leap, and all power to you – some of us need to go through traumas – so who am I to say, you have to have a cushion? But I don't want to see people suffering too much. People tend to get unrealistic expectations about what's possible in the first year or two.

Ashley Ryan, Founder of Her Smart Marketing, is a female entrepreneur who plays big and means business. She has consulted for Fortune 500 companies, bringing in 6 and 7-figure revenue for her clients through simple, un-complicated, savvy marketing systems.

Bruce W. Spurr began his entrepreneurial life in 1998, founded a dot-com start-up in 1999, and eventually turning his start-up experience into a business and marketing agency in 2002. Since then, he's served hundreds of clients, from Fortune 50 to start-ups and solo-preneurs alike. In that time, he helped 33 clients multi-million dollar businesses, added tens of millions to the bottom lines of others, and helped notable non-profits raise funds and build awareness of their causes.

YOUR NEXT STEPS

To learn more about Ashley and Her Smart Marketing, and to find out if marketing management is right for you, grab a free consult at www.HerSmartMarketing.com.

Ashley & Bruce also host a weekly livestream show on Facebook. Unstoppable is a "must-experience" for business owners and entrepreneurs. To join their tribe, sign-up at www.unstoppable.live.

CHAPTER 13:

GISELLE TONER ON TRANSFORMATION THROUGH COACHING & YOGA

Interview on Your Success Path Live – February 8, 2017

Could you share with us a little bit about your background and what got you to where you are today?

I had a very turbulent life, growing up. I needed to find ways to cope. As a young girl, I happened to be fortunate enough to be drawn to yoga and I made it my lifelong passion. I was a paralegal for many years. Talk about turbulence, that's one of the most turbulent professions that you could ever be in, so I needed a way to stay grounded, stay focused and stay centered. Yoga really helped me tremendously to go through a lot of the turbulence not only in the workplace but in my personal life. As a result, more and more it became my primary profession. Then I became a certified life coach, 10 years ago. Even more recently I got even further knowledge and education with the Robbins-Madanes organization. And Deepak Chopra – back in 1998 I learned personally from him all about perfect health courses and Ayurveda. So here I am today.

How do you integrate the discipline of yoga with that of the life coach training that you do?

When I was teaching yoga, I became a certified teacher. What I was finding was my personal clients weren't just there for a physical makeover or change. They were coming to me and they were getting on the mat and they were eventually bearing their souls and telling me their problems. I realized that there was a really big need for something much deeper than just taking them through physical poses. The ancient science of yoga is a transformational experience all by itself. But I found that when I was combining that with empathy and life coaching skills it was making women experience transformations that I was totally shocked by. They were taking their own levels so much further as a result of both of those modalities being combined.

Today that's what I do, I combine the best of yoga and the best of life coaching and I help people make major changes in their lives. It was just one of those organic transformations. It wasn't something I was looking to do, it just kind of happened.

What are the struggles that your clients are facing?

One of the most important things that happens to someone when I start working with them, when they start learning these deep secrets, is they have more control than they know. Unfortunately, they have given their power away in many areas. Whether they've gained too much weight, they're in a bad relationship, or they're in toxic environments with other people. What they don't know is that they have a lot of power and they just forgot and they don't know how to gain it back. What yoga does is it exposes the weaknesses in body, in mind, in breathing and in all the other areas that we have. It exposes weaknesses so we can start to strengthen the areas we need to. The same thing with life coaching. When they start to realize the power that they have, that's when the magic starts. That's when the fun starts.

Is there any age that's too old to start yoga?

Absolutely not. You can start yoga at the age of 79, 85, it doesn't matter. Because yoga is not just a bunch of physical poses. We don't have to become gymnasts. We don't have to become Gumby. Yoga is such an internal transformational process, and it's so amazing that when people start to get into it they say, gee, I wish I'd found this when I was younger, but I'm so glad that I found it now.

I'm thinking about the challenges we're facing today in society. It seems there's a lot of anger out there bubbling to the surface. It seems we need an outlet to turn that off. Is this something where yoga will play a role?

I'm going to give you one thing that is very profound. When people start reacting the way they are reacting, that is coming from fear, fear of loss. When we have a fear of loss in any area, whether it is loss of your dignity, loss of your power, loss of your home, loss of your freedom, that is the fear that fuels all of this anxiety and it just grows like cancer. When I start doing that, my friends start hearing it and they chime in and before you know it the entire country and the entire world is in an uproar.

It's all fear-based. When we start realizing that we do have a choice in not allowing that fear to take a hold of us, things change dramatically. It's easier than most people think, it really is. Fear causes anger. Fear causes every problem imaginable. So we learn how to stop the fear and things start to change. There are a couple of other things that are important, but that's one of the main components, fear.

Share a little bit about handling conversations that are difficult or toxic.

A lot of this stemmed from when I was working in the corporate world for many 30 years. I was a paralegal, working for probably one of the biggest firms in Philadelphia doing a lot of plaintiff's work. And I climbed up to a pretty high level quickly because I was a hard worker. I was finding myself in situations with people in the office, especially other women, who were not happy that I had the kind of status that I had and there was a lot of jealousy and a lot of back stabbing and things that were just really painful for me. So through the years of pain that I went through and having no friends whatsoever in the workforce, I started to realize that there were certain steps that I was taking to help myself move away from the toxic people.

I came up with five basic steps you can take to quell the craziness from people that are angry or toxic around you. I used five letters, Q.U.I.E.T. The first one is the letter "Q" and that's the word "quiet". Let's just say you've got this toxic person attacking you and making you feel terrible. They may be coming after you with some covert kind of negativity, or they may be outwardly blasting you: "What did you do?" or "It's your fault" or whatever it may be. The first thing to do is get quiet. Resist the urge to go back at them because you need to gather your thoughts.

Next you are going to do a breathing technique called Ujjayi breathing, and that's the letter "U". All you're doing is inhaling deeply through your nose, bringing that breath into the bottom of your lungs, a deep breath, and on the exhale through your nose, a little slight tightening of your throat so that you hear a whisper on the exhale. It sounds like the ocean. That's just enough to allow you to calm yourself down. If you don't know how to do that, just breathe normally, but deep breaths.

The third letter is "I". What you're going to do with that letter I, is you're going to say to this person, "I'm sorry you feel that way." What that's going to do is, number one, not make you wrong because you're saying, "I am putting it back on, you have the problem, but I'm sorry you feel that way."

Number 4 is the letter "E" which is empathy. When you say, "I'm sorry you feel that way," you are starting to feel some empathy for that person, giving them the moment that they need. Maybe they'll calm down. But the other important thing about that letter "E" is, when you give them that empathy, you do not try to fix them. You do not want to feed into it by saying, "What do you need from me? What can I do for you?" because you are putting it in their corner. They are responsible for themselves. You cannot fix them. You can only take care of you. This is really for you. What you're doing is giving empathy with no resistance. You don't want to resist them, because that gives them the ability to come back at you again.

We've got to avoid going into our own threat anxiety defense dynamic.

Absolutely, because they have a lot of anxiety going on and nothing will make them feel better than to know that you are feeling sick too. You don't want to give that to them.

Fifth is the letter "T". This is where you transition away from that person – if you can, physically. But if you can't move away physically, if you're in a closed space, in an office, you need to transition in your mind. This is where it takes psychological strength and emotional mastery, which may take some coaching to get yourself strong enough. That sometimes is one of the most difficult things to do, especially if it's with a spouse. You're married to that person. You are in the same house, you are living together, but you can learn to focus truly on yourself, because you cannot change another person, you can only change you.

Now this is very important. If you cannot transition away with your mind because this person is truly toxic, you may have to make the tough decision to either quit the job or end a relationship. There are people that are that narcissistic and that damaged in our lives. We may have to make the painful decision to break it totally. Hopefully it won't have to get to that point, but you may have to and that's a tough call.

Handling difficult conversations, managing ourselves in the moment is really a complex puzzle. We have to find a way to manage ourselves.

I agree. And I have to tell you that self-mastery is the key. Self-mastery is physical, it's mental, it's emotional and it spans everywhere. It's in your personal life, in your business life. Self-mastery is something that every one of us can get better at. There are certain things that you can do to make a difference. It's not as hard as you think but it does take the willingness to be open-minded. It really is amazing, because when you have self-mastery you don't become over-reactive. Everything is taken in the proper context, knowing that you have a lot more control that you even know. Then the fear melts away.

I think now more than ever we have to learn these techniques, because unfortunately, I don't see the tide turning where all of a sudden we're all just arm in arm singing campfire songs.

But that would be wonderful. You know something, Howard, it starts with the individual. We each have to take responsibility for ourselves and our own health and our own welfare.

Giselle Toner has over 30 years' experience teaching women and men how to increase their energies, physically, mentally and spiritually, through the ancient science of yoga, and to enhance their self-worth, personally and professionally through her Strategic Life Coaching Mentorship Programs. She's also a certified "Perfect Health" educator, having been trained personally by Deepak Chopra, M.D. and David Simon, M.D. in 1998. She currently holds retreats in various tropical destinations to teach "The Successful Goddess Blueprint," a training course that helps women Ignite Their Value in all aspects of life, and is a pubic motivational speaker.

Giselle is also the creator of two ground-breaking training programs: "The Abusive Relationship Trap" - 10 Lesson Training and Coaching Course to Help those in Pain from Toxic and Abusive Relationships; and the "The Successful Goddess Blueprint" Training and Coaching Course for Women who want to Ignite their Value, Physically, Mentally, Spiritually and Professionally.

YOUR NEXT STEPS

To learn more about Giselle and her work, visit her website at www.GiselleToner.com

---

CHAPTER 14:

TANYA LACY ON THE STORY LEADERS TELL

Interview on Your Success Path Live – February 14, 2017

Tell us about how you got to where you are today and the work you're doing.

Today I have the opportunity to travel the world, learning, teaching, and working with some amazing brands. I would say my ideal client, the one that I cherish, is Mercedes Benz. I've had my company for 20 years, doing this work in the leadership space, and that all sounds really powerful and amazing, but it wasn't always that way.

I'm someone who didn't even finish high school. Today I'm sitting in front of PhDs and MBAs in board meetings. I've really had a journey of redefining my own story and reframing who I am, and what my natural gifts and talents are. The work that I do today is not only technical or process oriented within an organizational experience, because I've applied a lot of these processes to myself and my own transformation.

I work with people about this balance of humanity and expertise, getting that balance right. The Intercept Experience is really about listening and hearing the story of leader. The story that that leader tells themselves has tremendous impact, not only on the people around them but also in the whole organization.

When did it occur to you that you may have a calling?

Sometimes you can be a victim of your own success and high performance. When I was 15 I was very capable at school, and then when it came to the time to make decisions about college or university I froze. It created a lot of anxiety for me. I didn't know which path to take. I was being pulled from mathematics to English to humanities, and was pretty capable across all of them. This was a frustration point for me. I had the idea that what I was learning would have no relevance in business. I'd always thought of myself as getting into business somehow.

A defining moment came where I was at this decision point, and a mentor of mine – he was married to my cousin – spotted me and said, "Look. You're naturally great with people. I'd like for you to come and work with me. Don't freak out about this decision. If you don't make it you can always go back to school."

I worked with him in the freight forwarding company at Melbourne Airport. I'm 15. Imagine this. He's giving me books to read: *The Power of Positive Thinking, How to Win Friends and Influence People, The Art of Selling Anything* by Tom Hopkins, *Think and Grow Rich* by Napoleon Hill. I think, for me, that was the first external validation.

Later on I was going through a very difficult time, and some of the most turbulent times are when opportunities pop up. I was going through a marriage breakup, and I did a lot of journaling. I got this vision, like an image of myself speaking in front of people. I didn't really know what that meant. This is in my early 20s. I took this concept to my partner and said, "Hey, this is what I believe I want to be doing. This is the direction that I want to take." He resisted and said quite derogatory things, doing the best he could at the time, but that was the grit in the oyster that made me rise up and say, "You know what? I'm going to do this."

I was in the process control engineering business, working for a Texan company in outback in Queensland. I was with this guy in his 50s, in his car. He was one of my branch managers that I was meant to be supporting and integrating into the American culture of this product we had. He was having trouble with himself. He was very angry, and he was driving really, really fast.

I was white knuckled and quite frightened. I spoke to him and said, "Hey, slow down." He said, "Don't worry, love. You'll see the dust of any oncoming car before we hit, so you'll be all right." I said, "You know what? This is an opportunity for us to unpack whatever's going on for you. Let's talk about it."

We had this deep discussion about his family, what was happening for him privately with his kids, with his challenge with his boss. He wasn't happy. It was in that moment that I helped him see things from another perspective and I thought, "You know what? I've got a bit of a knack for this," because at the end of it, he was telling himself a different story.

How did you begin to create a process out of this and evolve a business?

Well, after this experience I thought, "If I could help people get themselves in the right job, the world would be a better place." I did a stint in recruitment on the Gold Coast in Australia. It's this holiday paradise, and people would be escaping from pain. They would come into the office, and I would ask them why they were going for the role. Why did they apply?

They would say, "I've just broken up with my partner," or, "My last job didn't work out," or, "I've just moved." I realized that this was tumultuous for them, because if they hadn't paused long enough to actually heal and clear all that baggage, that baggage was going to land in the company that was my client. What I would say is, "Listen. You're a great person, but this is really bad timing for you. You know? You need to go and heal." They'd start weeping and say, "Thank you so much. Thank you. You're right. Yes. It's too early for me," but I wouldn't place anyone. I thought, "This is commercial suicide. What I need to do is now do this process with the CEOs and entrepreneurs."

I did my research. I'd decide I wanted to work with a certain company. I'd call and say, "Hi, I'm Tanya. I'd like to come and see you." And I would get them to make space with me. The very first question I'd ask them would be, "What is your vision?" Of course there's the private vision and then there's the larger vision of where it is that they want to go. I was 26. I thought if I could help business owners get happy, it would help a lot of people, because there's a responsibility in a business. If you're not happy as a leader, you're affecting a lot of people.

Working in recruitment I had learned the value of metrics and psychological profiles. The problem was I wasn't a psychologist. All that reading I'd done at 15 had showed me was that there were universal principles that applied to everyone for success in leadership. It didn't matter if you wanted a Ferrari, or you wanted to create an orphanage. I looked at how could I distill these qualities and apply some kind of metric, because men in particular like numbers. I knew that if I wanted quantitative insights, I needed to come up with some kind of measurement.

In partnership with some very smart people, I developed this leadership assessment tool. It's all about them, their team, their succession thinking, their leadership approach, whether they're a coach or a mentor, their self-awareness. We'd start there, spot gaps, and then go into a process of linking: "Here's your vision. Here's where you are. How do we get you from where you are now, to where you want to be?" That became the context for the sessions, and that's the Intercept Experience.

What do your clients look like now?

When we go and meet a team leader or a CEO, we ask this question: Do you accept the success of your business as a reflection of you? Because what we know is their mood is going to transmit. If they're grumpy, the business is grumpy. If they're unsettled, the business is unsettled. If they're happy, the business is happy. It's that simple. We want to test to see if they're really ready to adjust how they're showing up. That becomes our qualifying question.

Typically, people say, "We need to shift our culture. We're not retaining people. We're losing talent. Our morale is down. Profits are down…" These might be some of the challenges. Then what we do is we flip it and say, "If you really want to take charge of this situation, are you prepared to start with you?"

This is where it becomes pretty confronting, and that's why we call it Intercept, because we're saying, "You're telling me you want to shift your trajectory. We need to create that. This is the job of a leader. Does your vision match what you really want? Because your energy field is going to show up. How do you make sure you are transmitting positivity when you show up?"

This starts with the stories we tell ourselves. Are we using appreciative dialog that uplifts, or depreciative dialog that drags us down? We need to notice that, self-monitor and check the language we're using. In corporations and in other environments, perhaps it's because we don't always speak kindly to ourselves that we're prevented from naturally going to the positive.

In an environment right now of fear, uncertainty, and doubt – in turbulent economic times – a leader has to decide, "I'm going to create my own economy in here, and I am going to create appreciation dialog. I'm going to focus on what's working. And then when I see one of my team, I'm going to focus on what is it about them that I'd like them to appreciate about themselves?"

That person walks away uplifted, but not in a way that's dependent on that leader, like a hit of energy that's temporary and leaves the leader drained, but in a way that helps the person see themselves and hold their own confidence, hold their own value, and then go off and do the same. There's this ripple effect.

There's an analogy that I use. If we think about ourselves as four cylinders, mind, body, spirit, and emotion, what typically happens is when you walk into your corporate role, you're bringing your mind and you're bringing your body. A brand might be really caught up in how they look, or they're too technical, or too compliance driven, they lose the humanity piece. They only get 50% of that person showing up. They're not bringing their heart, and they're not bringing their energy.

A big part of our work is to say, "Hey, fire on all four cylinders. Bring all of who you are, be present to what you're doing, and if there's something that's disconnecting or that's a drain in dialog with another team member, to learn the art of communicating clearly and asking for what you want." That creates safety and positivity. But if the leader has not set up the environment properly, instead of people having the real conversation about what's going on, how they felt let down about a project, or whatever, that's when the water cooler talk happens, people talking behind the leader's back, trashing their own brand.

Talk about the importance of the stories leaders tell about themselves.

Okay. I was working with a general manager who was in his late 30s. He had left a country in Europe to be in Australia, and was a very successful athlete, a really high performer. In our conversations he had a big vision for what he was doing, driving success and uplifting people. In general terms he was quite a positive person, but he had an abrasive aspect. This abrasiveness came from his inner dialog. When we got to the bottom of it, one of his things that was driving him was fear and the need to prove himself. The reason was he didn't have any formal qualification. He didn't have an MBA.

In his brain he was telling himself, "I'm not enough. I've got to drive harder and further, because I've got to prove." This guy was running a 500 million dollar division, but somehow in his psyche he was focusing on what he hadn't done and what he didn't have, rather than what he had done, what he did have.

What I was able to do in this process was help him re-think his story, to look at all the positive aspects, all the highlights, all the natural talent that he had, all the things he could appreciate about himself that came easy to him. Then he was able to surrender the hard work and stop putting so much pressure on himself. This released some tension and he was able to rise to another level. He went on to do amazing things, groom his successor, and move on to his next thing.

Sometimes it takes an external person to show us ourselves. That's what you do, intercept the resistance.

There was a supermarket chain in the UK, and they had this line of shirts, and they couldn't move them. The executives would sit around at the meeting room and argue and strategize. There was a lot of ill will amongst this team. There was millions of dollars of this stock, and they had to move it. They were under a lot of pressure. A new leader came in with a fresh perspective, cleared the team, started having the meetings in a completely different room, brought in a different mindset, made space for a different story about the product, and within a couple of weeks, all the stock was moved off the shelves.

Somehow they associated success with this product, and how they were thinking about it shaped what happened in a tangible way for the whole business. This is what we've become conscious about. Is the dialog appreciation based, or are we focusing on the obstacle? Every day we get to choose that.

There's a whole piece here about shame. There are people who haven't dealt with the sense that they're not good enough. That blindsides people and puts a negative filter in, and then they end up hiding. Until you've worked through that aspect of your story and forgiven yourself or become at peace with your past, it's very difficult to break free and really bob to the surface. This is the work, too, being at peace with who you are as a human being, and accepting that you're not perfect. We're all striving for excellence. Being kind to ourselves in the way we appreciate who we are.

Tanya Lacy writes, speaks, and leads seminars on business leadership. She's an international businesswoman working with small family business to household brands.

She began her first coaching + consulting business working one on one with leaders helping them accomplish their goals and targets. This morphed into what's today known as the 'Intercept Experience'.

She develops programs, processes, and intellectual property designed to draw out the deeply held visions leaders have inside themselves, yet have difficulty conveying powerfully. Her work bridges this gap for the leader, translating and transmitting with clarity and simplicity into the hearts and minds of those in the business.

Today Tanya is all about positive dialogue and positive Influence. This shines through in her newly released book "Value Breakthrough How Helping Your People Deeply Appreciate Themselves Increases the Value of Your Company". The book contains proven appreciation dialogues designed to help business leaders increase the value of their connections between relationships, in the business, people and brand.

YOUR NEXT STEPS

To learn more about Tanya's work, visit her website at valuebreakthrough.com, and link to the free chapters of her book: https://interceptexperience.leadpages.co-free-chapters-vb/

Visit www.au.linkedin.com/in/tanyalacy to connect with Tanya on LinkedIn and www.facebook.com/ValueBreakthrough/ to connect with her on Facebook.

CHAPTER 15:

PATTI COTTON ON MAXIMIZING YOUR LEADERSHIP POTENTIAL

Interview on Your Success Path Live – February 1, 2017

Perhaps you can share with our audience some of your background and how you got to where you are today as a professional coach and entrepreneur.

I think maybe what's important as a backdrop is to understand that I grew up in an era where we were told that we could do anything, but we were subliminally discouraged from doing anything outside of some very restrictive norms. I wanted to be a child psychologist and then an attorney, but was discouraged both times – the second time actually shamed, being told that the men's wives wouldn't like it if I, as a female attorney, went on retreats with them. We're talking about the 70s. It was still alive and rampant: do what you want, but don't do anything except what we say.

It tended to confuse my identity, who I was and who I wanted to be. That's an important backdrop for my work, because later on I came to realize that that's exactly what you need, to know who you are and what you bring to the table, and to realize that in service of others.

During my early 20s I went overseas and wound up living there for a decade. My husband and I were in the Diplomatic Service for the Swiss government. It was a lovely life. It was a lot of fun. It was very exciting to be with other world leaders who were making change. That was greatly inspiring to me. I realized that people bring different gifts to the table, but whatever they bring, they can lead, which went against what we were learning in leadership.

I came back after a decade of living in Europe and went back to work in the corporate world. I was the chief development officer for a 5-hospital healthcare system, and ultimately we were raising millions of dollars. Again I started to become discouraged. It was very goal orienting, but it wasn't meaningful or fulfilling work after a while.

I popped over to Fielding Graduate University where you and I met. I did a master's in organizational management and development and really specialized in the executive coaching track. Things came together for me there. Taking your life experience and making meaning of it in a very structured way, allowing you to do that, is phenomenal. That's what Fielding helped me to do. I really got on fire to help others develop their potential to serve others in a way that makes meaningful impact.

That's a little bit of the background: leadership experience both in Europe and in the United States in different ways. I think I've played the role. I've been one of them. I understand a lot of the excitement and a lot of the foibles that could come along with such responsibility.

In the past, we learned a textbook definition of leadership that didn't take much account of what was in the heart. Working overseas, did you find this in the business culture across the board? Was it cultural dynamic – US versus Europe? Was it a function of gender?

I think the difference between Europe and America is Europe says, either you're on the track or you're not. If you didn't get on the track when you were young, you can't ever get on the track. Whereas America says, land of the free, do what you want at any point in time. We know it's not that easy, but it does open the gate to understand and embrace things like adult development.

There are definite cultural differences. I think the unifier in this is that once you get people to see they have more potential, they can start to think about leadership. It's the most exciting thing in the world to coach a woman from a country where it's predominately male based as far as leadership is concerned and to have them entertain this. Obviously, there are things that they have to wrestle with along the way, but that's your first step.

Is the 70s and 80s model of leadership still in place or has that evolved?

It's evolved somewhat. I think that most cultures still look at leadership as positional rather than relational. Here's what I mean by that. Are you a leader? People instantly think, are they at the top? Do they have a position of power by default because of the role? What I really like to deal with is personal leadership to help you get into greater positional leadership.

Personal leadership is something all cultures can easily embrace. Are you leading in your work? Are you leading in your life? Or are you simply letting the world wash over you? I think most of the world still hears the word "leadership" and says, "Oh that's a position." However, in America as we flatten the organizational model, we hear "leadership" and we start to think personal a lot more readily than perhaps other cultures.

Who are your clients?

In the early days, I coached people from Harvard, Coca Cola, Cisco, Girl Scouts of America, that sort of thing, but they were calling me in to help more with succession planning for greater leadership. It was very dedicated to just the top rung.

Lately, because of the flattened organizational model, that has descended to second level. There's a tech company in San Diego that's calling me down this week to work with four mid-level to top execs for succession planning in the next five years. I would never have been called in before for midline managers or executives. It would always be top. Now I'm going to be coaching top and second tier managers and execs because they understand that if you coach one person, you're coaching in a vacuum. If there's a particular behavior or something that this executive or leader is carrying out that's counterproductive, we can troubleshoot that and shift that. But if you want to make larger impact, create a culture shift of some kind, then we know that it's not going to be with one person. We're going to work with a few people at the top and then the next tier so that we can re-acculturate.

I'm doing a lot more top team coaching along with the top execs than I did before. A lot of non-profits see the value in that, but also the tech companies. There's a big one in San Diego that's calling me down this week. Where you see less is in some of the older companies that are slower to change. They will do it, but they'll do it for what I feel are mixed motives. It's, "How do we stay current and look good?" rather than "How do we really make bigger impact?"

Is this just about the age of the company, or is size a factor? And how open are family businesses to this approach?

Family owned businesses are a special animal. I do have some experience with that. I'm also a mediator and a conflict coach. Those two things come in handy most with the family owned businesses. You have a first generation that worked very hard to build the business: This is my baby, I found meaning in doing this so take care of it for me. Obviously I'm generalizing, but the general trend is that the second generation expects to ascend and take over. They simply inherit the position. That causes a lot of trouble, first of all because they don't know how to lead, and secondly because there may be those in there who are not family, who have the capability to lead, who get bypassed.

You have to work through a sense of entitlement. You have to create some self-awareness in what it takes to lead. With the family owned business, it isn't just coaching one individual. You might coach the top two or three simply because you want to create buy-in and consensus moving beyond just behavior change.

I can see the challenges, with owners who not only have to prepare for their exit, but prepare for the people below to take on new roles and responsibilities including family members. I suspect they don't realize it until they're ready to walk out the door.

It's true. What they've experienced before is perhaps poor communication and an abundance of conflict. Generally the children are already working in the business in some capacity. The fact that they're related to the boss means that the other people don't feel they can treat them as equals and they can't confront the problems in the same way. They can't take them to the boss.

In the takeover you'll not only see conflict, but a severe drop in productivity and people leaving. Those are the signs that tell you you're in real trouble. If you're a private business owner, you want to think ahead and say, we need to keep that bottom line sustainable and growing. I need to continue to scale. What can I do to set it up for success in next generation?

Do you have a process you start with as you begin a client engagement?

I do. I'll sit down first of all, do some due diligence and say, "What is it that you're looking to do? You brought me here because you say you have a problem. I want to hear about that, but first I want to hear where is it you want to be, what you want that to look like, and what is it that you want to do with the company."

Then let's reverse engineer back to, "What are you seeing today that's getting in the way? What kinds of behaviors? What kinds of mindsets? How is this manifesting?" Then "How is that affecting your bottom line? Are we looking at productivity? Are we looking at communication?" All of these things. Really getting a clear picture of where they want to head is important because too often the business owner gets caught up in the day to day and they forget the vision.

Then coming through to get a clear picture of success, bringing it down to specific goals. I will never take more than three goals. More than that is going to become very scattered. Then set the deadlines, timelines, and so forth. Once I have that, generally what I do is I say, "We need to invite the people in that you perceive need to get in line with this, and share this picture of success with them so they understand what you're expecting." That's a really window-opener, because a lot of times these people have never heard that before. That's part of the problem. If they don't understand what the expectations are for them, they're fishing around in the dark.

Down along the coast of California, I was asked to coach the second in command, an executive vice president who was going to become CEO of a large non-profit. The thought was that she didn't play well with others. She liked to do everything by herself. She got better results that way. Consequently, she wasn't talking to one of the other executive vice presidents whose department was affected.

I talked with the CEO, got the picture of success, got what she thought was standing in the way and also captured what she was willing to do in order for us to be effective. I sat down with the executive vice president and we developed a development plan. I call it a development plan for a purpose. I don't like to call anything performance plan. To me, that smacks of teaching a dog new tricks. It also stresses out the coachee, thinking, "I have to perform." This is really leadership development so I call it a leadership development process where we pin point how the behaviors are showing up that are not desirable, what it looks like for the behavior to be desirable, with the results. I help the coachee to get a clear picture in her mind as to what success is, what she's doing, how she's behaving because we're actually creating new neuro-pathways in the brain so that the brain can go toward it instead of holding you back.

When situations come up, we troubleshoot, we shift behavior, we go back, we redo, we go forward. That's basically the onboarding and the beginning of the process. The midpoint check-in to say, "How are we doing?" to the CEO. " What have you noticed?" Then coach to success over the next few months and sit down and assess with the key stakeholders as to whether or not they all agree that we've done a good job.

I propose six months. We needs six months or so because you didn't get this way overnight. It's going to take some time. So I will coach two times a month and I will give them some developmental work in between, so that they can actually flex that mind muscle.

Given our current President and the impact he appears to be having on women, minorities, people who are socially and economically challenged, how do we overcome what we're being introduced to from Washington?

I love that question. The first thing I would say is, don't abdicate your personal power. I think that there's been so much focus and attention on the election results, and rightfully so, that it has loomed incredibly large in people's minds. One person cannot make monumental change without followers. One man or woman does not a nation make or break. Yes, there are implications to the decisions that are being made now. But we must rise to our own personal best in our leadership. The larger the initiatives that we belong to, the greater the waves we make. I'm not calling for a revolution, but I want to say, don't abdicate your own power, because there are millions of people out there right now making huge differences that one person cannot change.

Patti Cotton works with high-potential female executives and professionals to engage, elevate, and equip them for greater leadership and outcomes. Now the Founder and CEO of her own company, she possesses more than 25 years of leadership both stateside and abroad, in diplomatic relations, and corporate profit and not-for-profit worlds.

During her tenure as chief development officer of a 5-hospital healthcare system, Patti designed a plan and led a team that raised more than $21.3 Million in 4 years – a feat that experts said could not be done. Leveraging this experience, she now helps women around the world to master their inner leader and executive presence for extraordinary results. An executive coach and Fortune 500 speaker, Patti delivers keynotes and briefings at regional, national, and international conferences; and company forums and retreats. She is a recipient of the United States President's Award for Lifetime Volunteer Service, and a part of all her business proceeds are dedicated to initiatives that provide alternatives to domestic violence.

YOUR NEXT STEPS

To learn more about Patti and her work, visit her website at www.PattiCotton.com. Contact Patti at patti@patticotton.com, follow her on LinkedIn at linkedin.com/in/patticotton, or on Twitter at PattiCotton.

CHAPTER 16:

LENI WILDFLOWER, PHD ON COACHING, WOMEN, AND LEADERSHIP

Interview on Your Success Path Live – February 27, 2017

Talk about what's happening with women and leadership.

First off, I'm not going to talk about women being superior to men, and I'm not going to talk about women as a category, because we're all individuals and some things that apply to women

apply to men also. I'm really just discussing issues from my own experience as a coach and out of the research I've done.

These are turbulent times. I'm an American but I live in London, so I've been watching the news. There are small impromptu demonstrations happening all over the country. So often the spokespeople are young women or women of color and I'm excited about this. I think our next president's going to be a woman. That's my hope and I'd like to see that in my lifetime. There's a way in which women have really taken hold of what's happening in reaction to the current administration.

Talk about the challenges women have had pursuing executive roles.

The not so great news is they've had challenges in the past and still have them. Women are the fastest growing sector of the corporate workforce. But they're still a minority group in the way they're treated. Since forever, corporate culture has been designed around traditionally male values, male behavior, male ways of working and talking. And there are certainly men who don't thrive in such a culture, but, overwhelmingly, women don't, and so if you act like a man, you're too assertive, if you act like a traditional woman, you're too passive.

Lots of the literature talks about this. Women walk a line between being functional in the organization and, at the same time, being themselves. The system is inadvertently stacked against them, not for malicious purposes, but because of the culture in which people have to operate.

I'll give you some of my history. I was part of the 60s women's movement, which came out of the civil rights movement and the student movement, where women were treated poorly. We were readers of Gloria Steinem and Betty Friedan, and one of the tenets was that women should be able to have it all. You think that you have to stay home because you have children? Bring the baby to work, and put him under your desk in a basket. Every two hours you can nurse him and then go back to your corporate work. Well, if you've ever had a baby, and you're nursing every two hours, you don't have a brain. It took us a while to work out that you couldn't have it all and meanwhile the attempt could drive you over the edge.

There's an article in a fairly recent Atlantic magazine by Anne Marie Slaughter, and it's titled "Why Women Still Can't Have It All." The story with Anne Marie is simple. She was working in the Obama administration. She had a huge job. She reports that Hillary, as Secretary of State, slept on the couch, got up at four in the morning. Anne Marie was doing all these things too, and was certainly very committed to the work. But here was her problem. She was a professor at Yale, and her sons were just moving into teenage-hood, and she was trying to fly back and forth between Washington and New Haven, Connecticut, and she really wasn't there as a parent. She said, "God, my kids are going to be gone in three years, and I won't have experienced it." So she quit. Now, she was considered, by many, a failure. First of all, they assumed she'd been fired, which she hadn't been. Then they judged for giving up that huge job, that opportunity. The point is you make choices – you make the best choice you can for you.

How do we figure out ways to help people like her, who are successful and talented, to make it work?

Well, obviously, there are all kinds of creative ways of working: partly at home, partly in the office, for example. Although women who work from home are still dealing with what they call the "time bind," doing double duty. Women tend to be more involved with the family if they have one. I can remember, when a child of mine was sick, half of my brain was there. I could do the work, but half of my brain was with the child. That's not true for all women, of course, and certainly a lot of men have stepped up, and are doing the cooking and childcare and loving it, so it's certainly not biologically determined.

But the other side of that is that for a lot of corporations these days there's an issue of engagement. How can we get employees more engaged? Now this plays to what's traditionally seen as a female strength. A lot of women are naturally more inclined to ask questions, to empathize, to seek consensus, which is exactly the way you promote engagement. There's no silver bullet for engagement, it has to do with understanding people's lives and being engaged with them.

Have men never learned it or do they just not do it as well as women?

I think men are absolutely capable of doing that, but if a culture says the way you get ahead is to be single-minded, focus on your own progress, go for the silver bullet, there's no encouragement for them to do it. The other thing is that a lot of women I have talked to say, look, I'm getting up there towards the top. I'm not going to wait to get pushed off, I'm jumping. I've had it. I don't want one more lunch where I'm discussing golf or work. Those are the only things that go on at a lunch meeting. I want to talk about literature, about movies, I want to talk about my kids, and all of these things are just not culturally done.

I've been reading Atul Gawande, a surgeon and a wonderful writer. There's a book he's written fairly recently on surgeons, and one of the things he says is that in order for a surgeon to survive, given the intensity of what they have to do, at lunchtime they mustn't discuss surgery. They have to talk about something else. Which is interesting because what he's talking about is absolutely a survival mechanism. But it's difficult in a corporate environment to say, you guys must discuss something else.

Are you talking about coaching people to take time to disengage?

Absolutely. Everybody is trying to handle the work-life balance one way or another, men and women. One time, I was working for a big television company, and I did a lunchtime series for women in their 40s and 50s who had young children, and all we talked about was parental issues. How do you stop this one from wetting the bed? How do you get this one to eat? These were high-level executives. Where else were they going to talk about this? Certainly you can't talk about it within a corporate culture.

But having said all this, I think there's another side to this issue. I wish I could say that women have some kind of enormous advantage at this point. They do have advantages, but I think it continues to be a struggle. The first woman to really talk about women's ways of leading was Sally Helgesen. Her book, *The Female Advantage: Women's Ways of Leading*, came out in 1990. She says in the book that there can be something called a leadership circle, that leadership can be more collaborative, and also that leadership can exist at different levels in the company.

When she first tried to publish the book, people said, look, no one's going to read this, it's way too personal. And, of course, it turned out to be a national best seller. Since then, the corporate world has come to have more appreciation for the personal. As she's said, these days even your bank manager wants to have a personal relationship with you. But she was already on to the fact that a personal connection is powerful in a corporate setting.

Is Sheryl Sandberg another role model for today's female leader?

Well, Sheryl Sandberg is the most popular. She proposes lean-in groups. A lean-in group really is women talking about how they can support each other in the work environment, and I think that's great. I think a lot of women find these very helpful and supportive. Another interesting book is New Rules for Women by Anne Litwin. She says that women are often either connected to each other or embattled, on a personal level, at work.

One thing women can do is create a set of rules for a work group and another set for a friendship group, and keep these things separate. Litwin says, look, in a work group, you need to be able to criticize behavior, give negative feedback. You also need to stay on target with a task, and strategize to support each other in team situations. Lots of women report, and I've heard this lots: I have a good idea, and some man immediately repeats just what I said, then he gets the credit. With the backing of a female work team, one woman can present an idea, and another is ready to support and echo it, so that way women get the credit.

A friendship group is really an emotional support group. Friendship is very important to women, especially in a workplace where they are the minority. In the friendship group, any behavior is okay. This is where you can cry, this is where you can feel whatever you need to feel. I think it's a clever book, because she's saying that the same women can function in different ways with each other. But they need to know, are we doing work, or are we doing friendship?

Does this idea extend beyond our culture here in the US to European culture, Asian culture, Middle Eastern culture?

Well I don't know completely. But I worked with all the HR women in a factory in Dresden, and it was all very familiar. They do the work, and they keep getting more and more dumped on them. Part of it is they're polite, and they get hurt. Lots of women I work with say: I've had it. I'm tired of implementing something I don't believe in. I want to do something creative. I want to do something that I can be proud of myself. I want to start my own business, or I want to go into a business that's small enough where I can have more of an influence.

Three bits of advice. And the truth is these to apply just as much to men as to women. First, own your own mistakes. If you mess up and you own it, you immediately shift the entire energy. Male executives have been taught by the culture to never admit a mistake. So I want to say to women that as soon as you own it, you've created something really important. The second is forgive yourself when you forget to do something or don't do it right. I have to tell myself this a lot too, but what's so wonderful about being a coach and a coach trainer is you've got to deliver this information, you've got to tell people about doing this every day, so it forces you to stay present in the space, which I love. And three, it's not your fault. Now, I'm going to quote from a book by Williams and Dempsey, *What Works for Women at Work*. This is wonderful, I think:

"It's not your fault that the men in your company consistently progress up the career ladder more quickly than women do. It's not your fault that last year's reviews said you needed to speak up for yourself, and this year's says you need to stop being so demanding. It's not your fault that you came back from maternity leave ready to dive back in but found yourself frozen out of major assignments. And it's not your fault that the woman you thought was your mentor has been arguing against your promotion. Plenty of things may happen to you that are your fault, but gender bias isn't one of them."

How did you get into coaching?

I'd been teaching in the Master's program at Fielding Graduate University, in organizational management and leadership, and they asked me to design a coaching component that could feed into the master's program. I remember I asked the head of a coaching association, what's the research on the best coaching programs? He says there is none. I asked why. He said, "They won't divulge what they do, they're competitive." Then I go to an ICF meeting and somebody gets up and presents this big theory about how to coach and says "I invented this theory" and I'm thinking, "Who are you, Freud, Einstein?" I came from academia, so I knew that mostly theories come from somewhere else, they build on each other.

So, I developed this program called Evidence Based Coaching. Now I call it Knowledge Based, because there are several strains that feed into coaching that aren't research-based, but come from some place of accumulated wisdom, such as self-help movements and traditions of spirituality. The manual for that course led to a book called *The Handbook of Knowledge Based Coaching*, which I co-edited with Diane Brennan with lots of different contributors. It not only talks about theory, but also about how to marry the theory with the coaching engagement.

Then I wrote *The Hidden History of Coaching*. I thought about all the people that were back there, both the kooks and the geniuses. I had great fun researching it and hunting in used bookstores for books about these guys. What's very interesting is that how much collaboration had to do with this. I'm thinking particularly about what was happening at the Esalen Institute in northern California in the late 60s and early 70s.

I'll tell you, when I was in the civil rights movement and the student movement we had nothing but contempt for those people sitting in hot tubs and contemplating their navels, as we used to say, instead of being on the picket lines with us. I had to get past all that stuff and look at how this happened. And when you look at who was at Esalen, it's quite astonishing. All kinds of people showed up there – Rogers and Maslow, ground-breaking therapists like RD Laing and Virginia Satir, thinkers and writers like Huxley, Joseph Campbell, Ram Dass, Buckminster Fuller.

Tell us more about coaching in turbulent times.

A lot of us were shocked and distressed by the outcome of the election. One of the things I've been saying is that the biggest problem on the planet is our inability to speak to one another in a way that acknowledges differences, that observes points of view other than their own. And frankly we now have a president who has no ability to do any of that. What we do as coaches is, one on one, we teach people how to become more skillful communicators. And right now that's hugely important.

Leni Wildflower *has 20 years' experience as an executive coach, author and educator, working in the US, UK, Europe, China and Latin America. Her passion as a coach is to inspire clients to reach new levels of clarity and effectiveness.*

As an innovator and thought leader on coaching as a profession, a discipline and a craft, she developed the groundbreaking programme of evidence-based coach training at Fielding Graduate University in Santa Barbara, and co-edited the definitive The Handbook of Knowledge Based Coaching: From Theory to Practice. *Her recent book,* The Hidden History of Coaching, *explores the fascinating history of the theories and practitioners who contributed to what we now know as coaching. She is an expert on blended learning and online education.*

YOUR NEXT STEPS

To learn more about Dr. Wildflower, visit her website at www.wildflower-consulting.com/. You can also connect with Leni on LinkedIn at www.linkedin.com/in/leniwildflower/. And you can contact her at leni@wildflower-consulting.com.

CHAPTER 17:

BRANDY AGERBECK ON GRAPHIC FACILITATION

Interview on Your Success Path Live – March 1, 2017

Tell us something about what you do.

I am all about drawing as your best thinking tool. For the past 20 years I have worked as a graphic facilitator. When a company is having a strategy session or an annual conference or they're convening folks, and they're just trying to have a more engaging, productive meeting, they hire me to come in and be their visual support person. What that means is they put a giant sheet of paper up on the wall and I map out their conversation while they're talking.

In my first book *The Graphic Facilitator's Guide* I talk about graphic facilitation having three powers. The first one is a power of being listened to. I think this is by far the most universal thing about graphic facilitation. You have all these people coming into this meeting and they all have their own ideas in their back pocket. And once they share that idea it's my job to grab it and put it on that piece of paper. The conversation changes when everyone has felt listened to and they see their ideas captured. And they see all those ideas integrated, and connected, and the patterns found and the connections made. I joke that I'm a human validation machine.

How did you hone this skill of listening and synthesizing what's said?

I think that my background of coming up through a difficult childhood where I had to be alert, and I had to listen, and I had to watch the signals of what was happening in the family was a really strong training. I'm kind of an odd ball that got into this work right out of college. For most people it's a mid-career change. I have a very good friend named John Ward who does amazing work with kinesthetic and visual tools. And he joked with me that people don't start listening till they're 30.

I think that there is something that just happens as you get older. You become more receptive to what other people are bringing to you. I felt like I was able to hit the ground running just given what my experience was growing up. And the more you work the more you pick up on patterns of how things tend to go – things like cadence, knowing when somebody is mulling over an idea, when somebody's rising to a point. One of my strengths is I'm a super spatial thinker. So I'm always alert to visual and spatial cues. You can tell somebody is trying to connect to another person's idea. They'll lift up their voice and you can tell they're trying to make a point that's distinctly different or in contrast to something that's already been said.

So I think a part of it is the musicality of the way people talk and picking up on those signals. In the book I talk about listening with outsider ears. I'm hired to do this job. I'm not politically involved. I'm in a perfect position to really listen with open ears. And even though I'm the silent partner, it's still a very active role. Nine times out of ten I'm front and center in the room because 80% of what you're hiring me for is watching your conversation take shape in front of you live. It's much more the act and the facilitation in the moment than it is the artefact afterwards.

It's experiential. Number one thing I tell folks is don't just plop that drawing in front of somebody and say, "See, this is what we did." Because there's all this energy and experience embedded in the drawing that isn't there for the person who wasn't there in the room. So what I say is: be a good steward of the image. Walk somebody through the drawing and say what resonated most with you and where did you see other's voices.

And this is power number two, which is seeing and touching your work. There's so much meeting fatigue. It's like you go and people convene and they feel like there's a thousand other things they could be doing but they have to sit in this meeting. And then the meeting's over and it's like poof, it's so ephemeral. People talk to each other in a room together and then it's gone. I'm making that conversation physical. It's literally in front of them. They can't ignore it.

So it's really key that people see it happening. There's a very elegant partnership that happens, because the facilitator is facing the group. And they're watching the cues, picking up on transitions and repeating main points. And just by the virtue of the job my back is to the room most of the time. The best thing is when there's sort of that symbiosis between the facilitator and me. Sometimes there isn't a traditional facilitator. The client just says we need you. And I say as long as somebody is making sure this isn't a circus – people talking all at once – I'm okay.

Is drawing an underutilized communication skill?

I had the opportunity to do a TEDx talk a couple years ago. And the theme of the day was contrast. So in the beginning I talked about the work of Linda Kreger Silverman who was a child psychologist who studied learning styles of kids. Now I know at the moment learning styles are getting a beating. But in her model, which I believe truly in my bones, she found there were two types of learners.

Auditory sequential learners are good at learning step by step. They're good at listening. And then there are visual spatial learners. Those are students who are good at making connections between pieces. They tend to learn all at once. If you ask them to show their work it just comes fully formed as a whole thing. Not surprisingly I'm far on the visual spatial side of the equation.

In her work she found that 33% of people are strongly visual spatial and 30% lean towards it. That's 63%. But that's not how school is set up. That's not how most work places are set up. I get that text is this incredibly easy way to distribute information but it's not a great way of processing information, especially these days when we're getting more and more information coming at us. The idea of spatial drawing is you put an idea on the page, you're not making a list, going from left to right, top to bottom – you can place the next idea anywhere else on that piece of paper.

That's why I think it would be fantastic if very simple drawing, drawing as a process not as a product, could be taught younger. Not to draw your portrait, but simply to get those ideas out of your head and onto paper.

Is there a narrative element to what you do?

My colleague Anthony Weeks comes from a filmmaking, and narrative is strong in his work. Susan McCloud comes from a journalism background, and she's really great at weaving stories. So I see colleagues who really embrace that. But the way I think tends to be more abstract and conceptual. I think of the drawings more like maps.

Every time you're making a drawing you're making countless choices. So it's like what's the next point I want to put on this piece of paper? What scale does it need to be? Where does it need to be in proximity to another idea on the page? Am I using a color for a specific meaning? So in every one of those choices, you're making meaning for yourself. And it's not using a template. It's really being purposeful in each of those choices.

I'm lucky in the fact that even though this work has been around for over 30 years and I've been doing it 20 years it's still very new to most folk. Clients don't have a lot of preconceived notions. I set up very clearly that what I'm doing is responding to the group. So just for example let's say that you've got two different constituencies in the room and they're coming together for the first time. This is a great application of graphic facilitation. If this like two giant figures on the drawing facing each other, here are all the ideas around these folks and then here's all the stuff where they come together in the middle.

What do your clients look like?

There's a huge variety. I specifically don't put a client list on my site because I don't want anyone to filter themselves in or out. A lot of it is corporate. But it's been education. It's been nonprofit. It's been government. It's been new start-ups. One of the things this works really well for is the beginning of something, when you're trying to just figure out what is the scope, the objective.

One thing I'm happy about that last few years is when folks come to me and don't have an event. Events tend to break down into either conversations or presentations. The conversations are internal strategy meetings or maybe a brainstorming session. Presentations are things like annual conferences, when they have the speakers on the stage. My favorite out of those two are the conversations. That's where I can have the most impact. But this third thing has been emerging, which is like co-creation with the team. They say we don't have an event but we're trying to – we need a visual that supports what we're trying to communicate. I come in and I work with a small team. I'm asking a ton of questions – What's the tone? What's the level of information? Who is this for? – and crafting what that image is together.

Which connects to power number three, I suppose, the power of shared understanding.

Absolutely. My new book is about teaching everyone visual thinking concepts. The book is called *The Idea Shapers*. It's 24 specific visual thinking concepts. This is the power of putting your thinking into your own hands. So this really is about everyone learning to strengthen their visual thinking skills. And really breaking down the complexity of visual thinking into accessible winnable pieces. For example, there's the cluster – you've got similar ideas and you place them near each other – and the partner to that is the buffer, the white space around it.

What really caffeinates me is the idea of teaching everyone these skills. I teach a three-day immersive called the lab. That's just six folks so it's this beautiful emergent agenda where we have three days of getting up with big sheets of paper and mapping out things. What's really neat is just about half the people are graphic facilitators or want to be me when they grow up and half of them come from other disciplines. And they see how great these tools are for being analytical and strategic and critical in your thinking and synthesizing information.

I do interactive keynotes. I've been at the front of the room watching the good, the bad, and the ugly of speakers for 20 years, seeing the death by PowerPoint and listening to all those different kinds of styles and approaches. I love blending speaking, teaching, and facilitating. I work with a group and I do a little a bit of "sage on the stage" style, giving concrete tips, and then they go straight into breakouts and start tackling scenarios using those brand new visual tools. And it's so gratifying to see them immediately picking up on those nuances that, until you're introduced to, you don't know how to tap into.

Our culture is getting more visual. We know more than we think about how visuals work, but most of us have been consumers and not producers. So it's helping people realize there are simple ways you can start creating these images for yourself.

What's your latest project?

The next thing I'm working on – with this political climate we're in, which I don't want to talk too much about because it makes me crazy – is a series on how to make protest signs. That's visual communication. I can help people ldo that for themselves – whether they're making signs that agree with me or not.

Then April is the 5th anniversary of *The Graphic Facilitator's Guide* so I'm working on a video series geared to clients – Who the heck are we? How is it best to work together? What kind of questions to ask to find a good practitioner? – that kind of stuff.

What I hear back from my clients, which is so gratifying, is when they see they're working in a new way and they feel that qualitatively that event is different because I was there to help support them. That ability to synthesize and shape people's conversations is my biggest strength.

Brandy Agerbeck writes, speaks and teaches on the power of drawing as your best thinking tool. She celebrates twenty years as a graphic facilitator, mapping out her clients' complex conversations in live, large-scale drawings. She wrote The Graphic Facilitator's Guide: How to use your listening, thinking and drawing skills to make meaning. *Brandy follows this much-loved volume with a book for every visual thinker,* The Idea Shapers: The power of putting your thinking in your own hands. *Cultural analyst Patricia Martin calls it, "A new alphabet for the visual age."*

Blending her experience in speaking, teaching and facilitating, Brandy delivers interactive, customized keynotes and workshops. In her engaging and productive sessions, she demystifies drawing to develop everyone's thinking skills so your participants can learn more easily, reduce overwhelm, communicate clearly and think critically. Her signature workshop is The Lab, a three-day immersion into visual thinking, offered in Chicago and abroad. You can see her in action in her 2013 TEDxWindyCity talk, "Shape Your Thinking."

YOUR NEXT STEPS

To learn more about Brandy and her work, visit her website at www.Loosetooth.com. You can also follow Brandy on Facebook at www.facebook.com/loosetoothcom, and on Pinterest at www.pinterest.com/loosetoothcom/.

CHAPTER 18:

RON KRAYBILL, PhD ON PEACEBUILDING & MANAGING CONFLICT

**Interview on Your Success Path Live –
March 2, 2017**

*Tell us something about your background, how
you got involved in peace studies and conflict
resolution and how it has evolved for you.*

My story begins with having grown up in
a Mennonite family in Pennsylvania. The
Mennonites, as perhaps you know, are a
pacifist Christian group and have for
hundreds of years, taught against taking of
life or participation in war. So that teaching was very much with
me. But I think it would be safe to say that mostly what
Mennonites were about for many years was saying, "We will not
participate in war." In other words it was a negative statement. It
was not a particularly positive outreach in offering alternatives.
In the years when I was growing up, I think there was
increasingly a sense that to be relevant to the world we live in,
we need to be apprised of alternatives to offer.

I was very much interested in finding a positive way of
expressing my convictions. I was in seminary at Harvard
Divinity School in the 70s, in a time when there was racial
conflict there. There were people experimenting with skills that

had been developed in the business and management world, for resolving conflicts, particularly through the American Arbitration Association. They were experimenting with using various skills and techniques in the setting of racial conflict. I had the great fortune of being introduced to a guy who was a former labor mediator, also a former pastor, who was now working in school de-segregation conflicts in Boston in a very tense time. I did an internship with him, and I knew within a matter of days that was what I want to do. That sense of call has been with me ever since.

I've done a variety of things with that. I worked in my early career in church conflicts. I then went to South Africa at a time when there was a major political transition. I ended up in a major advisory role to the political transition in South Africa. I taught in university for many years back in the States. Then I worked in Israel and in Africa and in Asia and in international conflicts. That sense of calling has taken me many places. Even now in my 60s, I have a deep sense this is what I'm meant to do in life.

It has to be a stressful profession. How have you been able, as an innovator, leader, and educator, to stay so passionate about this work?

To survive in this kind of work, you have to enjoy the challenge of disagreement and conflict. I realized early in my career, that there is a significant portion of human beings who do not enjoy conflict at all. They just want to get out of there. People like that probably would not do well in this kind of work, because it would just cost them too much. I'm personally energized by conflict. If it's too loud and too noisy, no. But up to a point, I like the challenge of finding a way to bridge differences, and having the skills and techniques that we use in this trade is for me a great joy to bring those to people who are in conflict.

It's important to recognize that everybody has conflict. And that just because I work in it does not make me immune from it. It's a heck of a lot easier for me to mediate in your conflict than it is to be a party in mine. In that sense, we all are on pretty equal footing. I've had my own struggles with conflict in life. I've divorced for example. I say that just to be candid - I don't think we need to be perfect in order to be a resource. We just need to bring our whole heart in our intentions to what we are doing.

Reading your LinkedIn profile, I was intrigued by this concept of under the table or behind the scenes conflict. I was wondering if you could share a little bit more about that.

I often draw a diagram with arrows going across the table to point out that across the table is what everyone focuses on when there's conflict. We're thinking about "How do we get those people together across the table?" The truth is, as I've experienced it, particularly as you get to higher-level conflict, that often it's the conflicts behind the table that are the most difficult. So, for example, in South Africa, you would think it was a black/white conflict, and it was. But in the process of trying to negotiate that big peace settlement in the early 90s, the most difficult conflicts were those taking place within the black community as blacks were polarized about whether to negotiate with whites. There was some tragic violence that took place there in those years.

Israel/Palestine would be another good example where the Palestinians are deeply divided among themselves about how to deal with that situation. As are the Israelis, although probably not quite as bitterly so as the Palestinians.

So one of the big learnings for me as a peace builder has been that, if you want to make a contribution, you have to look at the whole picture, look at all the conflicts on both sides of the table. Maybe your best contribution will be resolving some difficult conflict behind the scenes that doesn't get a lot of attention but can really kill the whole peace process if nobody's working on it.

When negotiations are in progress, is it two or three people going into a room and just arguing it out? Or is it teams of people?

It's both. There are moments when, even in the biggest peace process at the highest political level, it comes down to two people sitting face to face or two small groups of people sitting face to face, particularly in the early stages. For example, when Nelson Mandela started negotiating with the white government, they prepared him for that in the sense that they began to interact with him, take him out of prison on short visits. He met with the State President of Israel a couple of times. So that does happen. Also if there's a crisis, sometimes the top guys get face to face. But for the most part, the big processes are more about teams. There are many issues that need to be addressed, so much technical knowledge required. One person can't master it all.

The other factor also is that you don't want to get all your eggs in one basket around the interpersonal dynamics of two individuals or four individuals. So the larger international processes involve teams fairly quickly.

What is your work focusing on today?

I can give you a very current example. There's nothing confidential about this. You may be aware that there's a peace process that's been going on for a number of years in the country of Myanmar right now. They achieved some of the early breakthroughs, as far as the major framework to be built. But the real hard work still lies ahead in terms of a lot of the issues that need to be resolved – economic allocation issues, issues of what to do with armed groups, constitutional problems that have not been resolved. All of that is ongoing at a national level. In addition, all the regions of the country will be affected by this. And there will need to be negotiations taking place in all the provinces of Myanmar, to work out, for example, what to do with the fighters who are still in the jungle in this particular province and government troops in place a few miles down the road.

There's a huge array of issues, and the number of facilitators who will be required just to facilitate those negotiations, by some estimates, are in the hundreds. So I'm working there as a trainer of facilitators. I go for a number of weeks every few months, and we do a series of intensive workshops on facilitating negotiations at these secondary levels.

In my early career, when I was working based here in the States, I was doing a lot of hands-on mediation and facilitation. But in the international world, it's more appropriate, not for me to be the facilitator of talks, but for people closer in to the conflicts situation – ideally nationals in the country where we're working or maybe regional organizations. And my contribution is primarily consulting and advising people like that or providing training directly to them. Or often it's training people in institutions and universities or other places, who will then be support people to the local processes.

Thinking back, have there been particular conversations you've had, when you've said afterwards, "Wow, we did good today"?

I think probably top of the list is one that happened in my years in South Africa when I came as an international resource person and was director of training at an institute in Cape Town. I was there for about a year before the peace process started in earnest so I had got oriented, and I had years of experience here in the States in the conflict resolution field. So I had what people were really beginning to realize that they needed. It was really exciting to give what I had. I worked with a team of people around me that we had funding to hire trainers and plug them in in various ways to this peace process that was unfolding.

One of the things I did, which I feel best about in retrospect, was after I had been there for a couple of years I began to have a troubled conscience. I realized that I now had a number of South Africans, whom I had trained and worked with as colleague for a number of years, who had developed tremendous confidence, who had all the skills that were needed to do the work that we were doing, including to be Director of Training at this institute that I was in. Here I was, an international in this position, and I remembered something that one of my early mentors had said to me. He said, "Ron, if you really want to be a peace builder, your goal always should be to work yourself out of a job."

I talked to the director of the institute. He was a man of principle. He understood exactly what I was thinking. We agreed I would resign as Director of Training and that he would work with me in finding other special projects. We did that, and a guy I had hired and trained became Director of Training and I began to report to him. That was something that I think said a lot to my colleagues, most of whom were black, in a time when whites had dominated things in South Africa and were happy to stay dominant. So I think it was deeply appreciated by my colleagues.

In the end it worked out great for me, because I got to do other work that was just as interesting. So in the end I didn't suffer at all, although at the time I wasn't quite sure what this was going to feel like, in all honesty. That's a decision which I still take pride in. It really sealed our friendship. We stay in touch even after many years. I would say the work in general in South Africa was to me tremendously satisfying, because there was a long period of time there where it looked like the process might fall apart. We had many crises when we really thought war could start any time, and somehow it all held together. Quite a few people died in that time. That's not widely known here. So it was not easy, but it did bring a significant change.

More recently I worked in Lesotho, which is a tiny country in southern Africa, supporting religious leaders there who were mediating between politicians. That was a really tricky and difficult task, because no one knew who I was. No one was sure if they wanted me around. There was a lot of suspicion and mistrust. For the first year I literally thought I'd probably go home with nothing contributed. I was working with the UN by the way. But I stuck with it, and we turned some critical corners.

These religious leaders began to meet once a month and gather to talk to about a plan. They put together a framework for negotiations between the political leaders. They agreed on a way to end the violence that had been troubling elections there for 30 plus years. And in 2012 we achieved a free and peaceful election. In that country it was the first time since independence in the 1960s that they had had a free and peaceful election. That was a very deeply satisfying experience because it was so hard, so nip and tuck for a while, but we came through it.

I wonder if you would talk a little bit about the Conflict Style Inventory? What is it? And why does it continue to be so useful today?

I started using a conflict inventory when I was in my early 30s. My mandate was to establish a network of conflict resolution, this was back in the early 80's, in a time when conflict resolution didn't mean much of anything to most people. And I was working religious networks at that time, and my challenge was how to help people get the idea of what this is about and get interested in it. I discovered that conflict style inventory is a fantastic tool to get people started on a journey of learning.

There are several of these around so it varies a bit, but in mine, and also in the Thomas Killman Inventory, there are 20 questions. So people answer these questions about how they respond to conflict. What they get back then is a score that says, well, you're preferred style of dealing with conflict is directing, which is pretty forceful and assertive. Or your preferred style of dealing with conflict is avoiding, which is basically getting the heck out of there. Or a mix of those.

I developed my own version of this starting in the 80s, because with the Thomas Killman in particular, I found in cross-cultural settings, I got a lot of complaints about the way it was structured. It was also pricey, and I was working in situations where I wanted to use this widely without always having to worry about busting someone's budget.

So I began to develop an alternative that is culturally flexible and priced at a reasonable level. In the current version, if people take it online, they get back a six-page report. It gives a rather detailed picture of their conflict style with a set of suggestions about the dangers of this style. The basic concept is there is no perfect style. The danger is that we tend to prefer one style more than others.

Let's take the directing style. Some people look at that and say, "Well, I wouldn't want to be a pushy director who insists on things." And my response to that is, really? Supposing your six-year-old son is walking with you on the sidewalk, and he sees something interesting across the street and he makes a dash across the street. Are you going to be an avoider or a harmonizer? I don't think so. In that moment, the only appropriate response is for you to be very assertive and grab that little duffer and hold on, even though he may not like you at all in that particular moment. Or if you are the captain of a sinking ship, you need to step in there and take charge. So the idea is that we can significantly improve our effectiveness if we look at our style and expand the range of styles that we use, and also understand how to bring the best out of other people.

What's next for you?

I'm in a major transition, because I hit mandatory retirement in the UN in 2015, so now we're back in the States, living in the Washington DC area. I expect to be active for many years yet so I'm figuring out the best way to do that. I expect to continue with the consultancies like the one in Myanmar for a number of years.

But one thing I'm particularly interested in now is serving as a resource to people who are themselves wanting to resource those around them in dealing with conflict. As you eluded to earlier in our conversation, we are in a time where there is a tremendous amount of mistrust and polarization not only in our society, in our world. When times really win, we could bring everything crashing down around civilization. Having spent decades in this field as a practitioner, my interest is in serving as a resource to others, who want to be practitioners and trainers themselves. I'm giving a lot of thought as to how to do that.

Dr. Ron Kraybill has been a pioneer in conflict resolution and peacebuilding since the 1970s. He facilitated the first restorative justice mediation cases in the United States in 1977 and was founding director of one of the earliest conflict resolution organizations in 1979, the Mennonite Conciliation Service.

Kraybill spent 6 years in South Africa (1989-1995) as Director of Training at the Center for Conflict Resolution in Cape Town. During this time he also served as Training Advisor to the South African National Peace Accord 1991-1994, and led a large number of workshops for negotiators in the national peace process.

In 2006 he established Riverhouse ePress (www.RiverhouseEpress.com), which markets his culturally sensitive Style Matters conflict style inventory to universities, trainers and consultants in 6 countries.

From 2007-2015 Kraybill worked as a peacebuilding adviser and trainer abroad. He worked in Jerusalem for the Quaker organization, American Friends Service Committee, and in Lesotho and the Philippines as Senior Advisor on Peacebuilding and Development for the United Nations.

Since 2015 he has lived in Silver Spring, Maryland, and divides his time between peacebuilding practice and Riverhouse ePress. Currently he spends about one out of every 4 months in Myanmar, training facilitators in the national peace process there.

YOUR NEXT STEPS

To learn more about Dr. Kraybill and his work, he blogs at www.KraybillTable.com. He can also be reached at ron.kraybill@gmail.com.

CHAPTER 19:

DR. MICHELE GUNDERSON ON THE POWER OF STORIES

**Interview on Your Success Path Live –
March 2, 2017**

Michele, I'd love to learn about how you got into this field of stories and working with other professionals how to use stories in their work.

I've been working with stories and words for over 25 years. It kind of shocks me sometimes that it's that long. Where I began was in the university and what I noticed was that so many students had a dream, they had a vision, but it really wasn't happening. They were so tight, they were so closed down, they didn't know how to make that vision real, how to say what they wanted to say, how to get it out there.

I was working with the students and helping them to find an opening. Then what I noticed was it wasn't really happening in my own life. When I left university I had a lot of different breakdowns. I wasn't making any money. What was happening to my relationship? I really had to understand how do you take this knowledge that was helping others and make it real in my own life?

I wanted to understand what makes a story embody? What makes a story align? What makes it real? What makes it move things in the real world? Once I started to investigate that, it was really fun, the things that started opening up in my business from not making any money, feeling lost, not reaching people, to starting to work with exactly the people I wanted to work with, helping them open up their lives, their businesses by looking at what was going on, both on the inside and on the outside, what they were telling other people.

Talk about story. What do you mean by it?

Here's the thing, sometimes people think the story's that one piece where I'm saying my bio or I'm on stage. It's nothing like that. Story is everywhere in our lives. Right now we're telling stories. Stories are the things that tell us how we move from one state of being to another, how we get from here to there.

As entrepreneurs, as visionaries, we're really interested in change. What is it that creates change in our clients? What creates change in our lives? What creates a growing business? The story is the mechanism by which we understand change, and when we can understand and enact that power in our lives it changes everything from how we treat our team, to how we talk to our kids, to what we say to clients in sales conversations, to how we meet people at events, to what we say on stage. These are all stories, stories about change.

I teach people about genre. Sometimes we go, wow, I got this project and it started out really well, but man, something happens. Every time. Something goes wrong and it gets derailed. All the energy sinks. What I would say is that's living in the wrong genre. That's where you live your life as a tragedy. We don't even know we're doing it, but it cans everything.

I'm wondering, is there a point of insight that people have, when they realize they're telling the same story over and over again, and it's not getting them anywhere?

Often we don't even know that we're telling the same story over and over again. We think it's some other kind of problem. Maybe I don't have enough time, maybe I don't have the right team, maybe people don't understand me. These are all story issues. We're always living in a story of our own creation. We don't even know we're doing it.

One of my students had all these outrageous goals. She wanted to do so much and had already built a lot, but wanted to build more and wasn't getting there. She came to one of my retreats. She's a young, beautiful woman in her twenties. You'd never guess that she'd already accomplished so much. We started to uncover it and she had this story running about aging. You'd have no idea looking at her. It's like, "I've got to go faster. My 30th birthday is approaching." As we started to uncover that and saw the rush in her life, it was always like moving through things too quickly, then she could never get there. Once we sussed out that story it was the big part of the work we did. She created these outrageous goals. She met them all before the beginning of March, her year-long goals. Now her problem was, "Well, now what, Michele? I don't know what to do next." That itself could become another disempowering story.

How do we gain insight into our stories?

You need some kind of mirror, some kind of community that can reflect it back to you. Journaling can help. You've got to have some way to look inside. One of the things I want to get across is that there's no place outside story. Right now we're telling stories about stories. When you're talking to somebody you're telling a story. When I see that I never step outside of it, then I can start to look for the stories that are around me. What I'm wearing, the ways I'm walking, who I'm talking to – I can start to track that.

Stories are everywhere. Some of them are empowering and some are disempowering. To even realize that is monumental, because that track that's running inside we don't even know. I don't realize sometimes that I have a choice about the things that are being said inside me and that my body reflects too. I could have a happy track inside my head for instance: oh, I'm really so smart. I love what I do. But my body is telling a different story.

What I'm hearing is the idea of story and the impact it can have on us is complex. How does that show up in organizations? Do organizations have stories?

Absolutely. It's different for entrepreneurs than for somebody working in corporate. As an entrepreneur, you need to create all the stories – for the team, internally for yourself, and so on. In corporate the story is given to you and you need to work within those official stories, but there's all these other layers of stories going on. If you are managing in corporate you have to be able to know what the levels of stories are and then be able to intervene.

First, you've got to listen with a subtle ear to what the story really is. I point to someone like Martin Luther King or Gandhi. What gave them their power? They told a story so empowering that everyone came on board. Everyone became engaged. You have to know about the structure of story and be able to engage it internally and externally for your people. There's a lot going on, but it starts with really understanding how stories work.

Can you give some examples of the impact your work has had on some of your clients?

The people I work with all have a gift to give and it really matters that they get it out there. They're feng shui specialists and fitness trainers and consultants and a whole range of things. They've got a vision. Just to mention one of my students. Bonnie. She was doing some really great work, moving the needle for some people, and she's making a few hundred dollars and doing okay. We did some work around what exactly is the story around your price point? What do you need to be offering this at? There can be a disempowering story: "Well, a lot of people do this" or "I don't know if they can afford it." Stories about other people's stories, even. It can be so disempowering. And as we worked just to figure out what the price point should be, she went from making a few hundred dollars here and a few hundred dollars there to really engaging with her clients. She had her first $36,000 month out of nowhere. She had never done anything like that before.

For me, it's not about the money. The money is just representing the energy that's going out there in the world. Her work literally saves women's lives. She helps them tap in. She's a beautiful speaker. She went from not having offers to speak of. This offer landed in her lap – she's speaking in front of an audience of 300. The person who's speaking beside her holds her up as the example of what it is to be aligned, what it is to have a message, what it is for your work to matter. All that coming from just tweaking a story around price point. Tweaking a story around value.

I was working with a speaker and she wasn't getting the results that she wanted. She realized that the outward story was really good. The story inside didn't match it. As she started to align those two stories people started to hear. Her message started to get out there in whole different ways.

Another one of my clients works in a Montessori school. And the way that the kids started listening, the way the staff started interacting – whole different ways once she started to understand what stories were being told and how she could tweak it so that overall mission of the school could shift and change.

I want to emphasize this point about stories – they're right in the body too. One of my students, all I did was I helped her stand differently. She came back a couple weeks later and she's like, "Michele, everything has changed. The way people talk to me, the way people look at me, the way they're listening, the way my spouse is listening to me. Everything changed just from that."

When I go to a networking event, that's a lot of fun because people just say a few words and they don't know that they're telling me a whole volume of stuff. I have the ears to hear it. But so does everybody else, they just don't know that they do. People are attracted or repelled and there's a whole level of story that's going on about the body. There's some wonderful work by a man named Dr Paul Zak. He's a neuroeconomist. He says that when we tell a story it's connected with a release of neurochemicals like cortisol and oxytocin and it moves people to act. When they don't tell a story they don't act. This is really important for managers, corporations, for entrepreneurs. It's about how does change happen. How do we move people to do something?

You were saying earlier, "Well, this is really complex." That itself is a story. What if we said, "Well, this is really simple?" What if there's some key components that, when I understand it, could really move the needle of my business? I can jump from making a few hundred dollars to $36,000 in a month. I can jump to having my team actually be on board. I can have people pay me more than I ask. I can have people really moving the needle in their lives and touching others. What if it could be that simple?

Dr. Michele Gunderson, "The Breakthrough Story Expert", teaches visionary messengers how to tap into the secret power of story to catapult both their businesses and their lives. A bestselling author and former university instructor, Michele helps heart-centred entrepreneurs create empowering stories in every aspect of their businesses, from speaking and networking to managing a team to getting the words out. Her clients go from not knowing what they want to offer to easily creating five-figure months, or weeks, in a business they love. When you discover your own empowering story with Michele, you can learn to play more, have fun, create a profitable business, and powerfully share your gifts with the world.

YOUR NEXT STEPS

To learn more about Dr. Gunderson and her work, visit her website at www.MicheleGunderson.com.

CHAPTER 20:

DONNA CERIANI ON LEADERSHIP COACHING

Interview on Your Success Path Live – March 2, 2017

Could you begin by painting a picture of where you are today?

I love that you and I have similar backgrounds, Howard. When I first started my career, I was in technology. When I learned to be a programmer, it was in the age of key punchcards and big IBM mainframes. I loved the excitement. I was an early lover of technology at age 19 when I got my first job as a programmer. Then, through the years, my love became more about motivating teams – big projects, big corporate initiatives to lead teams to create transformation in the company.

I got to a point where what got me excited wasn't the piece of technology. I got more excited about seeing my teams grow and thrive. So my focus became more about leadership, training, personal development. My company transferred me to Singapore and the job was to build out bench strengths in the region so we could prepare for growth, so that as sales would double or triple in Asia, I would have the right people in the right places. But what I found myself doing most of the time was coaching.

As I went from Japan to Hong Kong to Sydney to Manila and the Philippines and so on, I was really coaching people, coaching my leaders, coaching the individuals. I found myself taking almost everybody that I could to Starbucks and saying, "So, what do you really want to do and what makes you happy? Where do you want to grow?" And so I said to myself, when I get back to the US, I want to learn to be a coach. I want to strengthen those muscles and take formal training.

I got transferred to Manhattan. My job was to transform the team in terms of its role within the company, its efficiency and productivity and so on, but I took all my vacation time to go to training courses. Then I'd come back to the workplace and anybody that worked with me or for me, I would sit down with them and I would practice my coaching skills because I wanted to be a better leader, and ultimately I knew my transition would be to leave the company and become a full-time coach but, as you know, it's not something you just do overnight.

When I was in New York, I got to the point where the big goals that I needed to accomplish were completed. And when it comes to something that's routine and operational, I don't thrive in that environment. I thrive when it's a big project, something we really need. I call it inspiring transformation. I knew that the time was getting close for me to move on, and I had the opportunity to leave with a package, because you can't just leave a corporate job and the next day say, I'm going to be an entrepreneur, especially if you're earning good money, you have a mortgage, you have rent to pay. It took me a few years of zigzags to do it full time. Because people ask me, "Oh, Donna, how'd you make the leap?" Well, it wasn't overnight. I planned it for a very long time and there were baby steps in between.

I had the opportunity with one of my first corporate clients for consulting, to come on board as Chief People Officer and, basically, help architect company culture. We ended up winning an award. I'm not an HR person by training, but that gave me an opportunity to fill in pieces of my background. It was a fantastic experience and I use everything I learned with my clients today.

One of the things I found when I made that leap to start coaching full time was how much I was learning by serving my clients. I had a lot of clients because I was charging only to get the coaching experience, not for profit, and was putting all the pieces together on what it takes for someone to feel satisfied and successful on their path. I started putting together a step-by-step program. I realized that, for every client I had, I was filling in a different piece of the puzzle.

Today, I serve different audiences. One is individuals for coaching and the other is corporate clients, but because of my background I know that I relate better to somebody who's in technology or financial services because I was in technology for thirty five and financial services for fifteen, so typically they come from one of those two backgrounds.

When I walk them through a process of how to get clear on what they're good at, what they really enjoy, what their vision is for themselves, and then clarifying their personal brand, I'm helping them, like you say, Howard, on their path to success.

Tell us more about the system you've created.

One of the challenges I had in the beginning was, what do I want to be known for and what would I want those clients to come to me for? For coaching, it's a technology or financial services leader who's ambitious. They want to either get a promotion or be seen as a more inspiring leader, so they have leadership aspirations or maybe they're already in a new role and they want to make sure they're successful.

Then a smaller number of people are at a crossroads in their career. They're not sure which way to turn. They need clarity and guidance on how to make some career choices. Usually that's on the individual side. On the corporate side, I usually work on company culture, leadership development and engagement. But if the thing that shows up for you – the phone call, the email – connects and resonates and it's something you'd love to work on, you know you've done a good job in getting the message out on what you deliver. It's an affirmation that you've gotten the word out and it's a clear, consistent message. So if someone said, "This is a small tech company, 200 people, going through a lot of change, wants to focus on company culture and employee engagement. You know who does this? Donna Ceriani." Then I get that referral that tells me I've been clear on what I offer.

With my individual clients who are leaders, not entrepreneurs, I always ask them, regardless of why they're looking for coaching, "What do you want to be known for?" Because let's say they really want to be known as a leader who develops their team so that other people can't wait to work for them. How are they acting, presenting themselves, showing up so that that personal brand is authentic? And that's their reputation and then they're attracting what they really want to achieve. It absolutely correlates to anyone, really. What do you want to attract in your life? And how are you behaving and presenting yourself so that you're at the top of people's mind if those opportunities come up.

Do you have a system when you're working with client?

When someone wants coaching, the first step is, what are their goals? Then I reach into my toolkit and pull out what's appropriate. For some people, it may be one-on-one coaching. Based on their leadership aspirations I might do an emotional intelligence assessment. It might be either a self-assessment or a 360. Because 85 percent of your success as a leader is how you're showing up and interacting with people. That could be number one. Depending on what they present as a goal, I have a step-by-step program where it walks people through discovering their strengths, passions, and values. They create a vision. They do some work on their personal brand. I think of it as a foundation.

I've named all my programs based on my snowboarding passion. I've been snowboarding for almost 20 years, but I didn't even start until I was 39. If anybody ever says, "I'm too old," I go, "Well, I don't think so. You're never too old. I use the term acclimate to accelerate because you don't just show up as a leader and go right to the top of the mountain, up above the clouds. You're going to get altitude sickness. You haven't done the basics, you didn't prepare yourself. You've got to acclimate first.

To continue your snowboarding metaphor, if there was a client that was the perfect run for you, what would they look like?

First of all, I love working with people who are not only ambitious but who love to learn. I've seen people at all levels of an organization, if they're open-minded, willing to grow. I think mindset is really important. They're ambitious, they want to do more, but they have a mindset of investing in themselves.

I don't know about you but, if I'm coaching someone who doesn't want to read an article, look at a book, listen to a podcast, they don't want to do anything that's actually a learning activity, then I find that's difficult, because learning is one of my strengths and it's something I'm passionate about. If someone has a passion for learning, they're ambitious and, also, they really are authentically, genuinely committed to creating a workplace for their teams to thrive. They recognize that if they become better it's that rising tide lifts all boats. If they become a better leader, then they can inspire and help and companion their people. Those are some of the ingredients that, when I hear them, are music to my ears, because they have a vision bigger than themselves and I think that's exciting.

Now, if you help those leaders, it's that ripple effect. You're helping so many other people. If they learn those secrets for themselves – how to get your best results doing what you're good at, being clear in your brand – they can translate that to their team.

An ideal client for me is somebody mid-career. They have at least ten, fifteen years' experience, maybe more, and they're at a crossroads and they realized that the money is great but that's not providing them a level of satisfaction. I've never had someone come to me and say, "I just want to make more money." There's usually some burning desire. Like, for me, I walked away from a huge salary in tech and financial services, more money than I ever thought I'd make. And I walked away from it because, frankly, I was miserable. You know, it affects your health, right?

Yes, it does. I can attest to that. So what's next? If you could look at five years from now? I know you're going to be shushing down the mountain again on that snowboard of yours.

First of all, I know that I've created a program that is incredibly impactful for my clients. Between the coaching and the program, I've had clients come back to me when they finished the program and they feel as though they've made a jump in their career they thought would take years to make. They've made it fairly quickly because once they got acclimated and they got these pieces in place, they were able to accelerate some career moves. I've seen the validation through the years that this works. So five years from now, I would want to spread the impact of the program and have a much bigger impact.

My five-year vision is actually more personal joy. I would love to have an integrated event, maybe a three-day leadership event where we are in the mountains. Some of the work you do before breakfast, but you go out into the mountains, get fresh air and exercise, get inspired, then you come back and do some more work. It takes it out of a corporate Hilton, the stuffy classroom, and gets you out into nature. Because I really feel like we're at our best when we're in nature, getting exercise with other people. That's my vision.

Donna Ceriani is a Leadership Success Coach who helps leaders get their best results, advance their careers and create a workplace for their teams to thrive. Prior to becoming a coach, Donna held senior leadership roles for more than 25 years in technology organizations in the U.S., Europe and Asia in the financial services, technology and health care industries.

Donna was recently the Chief People Officer for SmartBear Software, winning a "Best Place to Work" award. Prior to that, she was an Executive Director for Global Client Operations for a company owned by Thomson Reuters and the DTCC, living in Boston, NYC and Singapore.

Today, she balances her time between working with individual leaders to accelerate their success and with corporate clients on shaping their company culture, leadership development and employee engagement.

YOUR NEXT STEPS

To learn more about Donna and her work, visit her website at http://successcompassstrategies.com/. While you're there, take the Altitude Assessment, and find out your Success Compass readiness.

A Message
From Howard

To everyone that made the decision to purchase this book, thank you. It means a lot. I hope that you found the insights and practices helpful as you grow your learning edge, and continue on your path to business success.

My own takeaway from setting out on this book authoring adventure is just how many ways entrepreneurs and coaches are serving their ideal customers and clients. Each of us is on a different path to business success. The needs from one business or leader to the next are very different. For me, diet and exercise, yoga, and discovering more about the stories we tell, are important to my own ongoing professional development and well-being.

Whatever your path to business success looks like, my encouragement to you is that you be open to getting just a little uncomfortable. Surround yourself with others who are on their own path to business success; I can't speak highly enough about the value I have found in joining and participating in mastermind groups. I encourage you to read *Think and Grow Rich* by Napoleon Hill (Highroads Media, Inc., 1960), to learn about mindset, and the power of masterminding.

If your path to business success includes developing your Individual and team leadership skills, know that there is no shortage of resources, material, and opinions. As of this book's publishing, there are over 32,000,000 returns when searching for leadership development on Google. Your biggest challenge will be to find the theorists, educators, practitioners, and models that are right for you and your organization. My advice is to read as much as you can on the topic of leadership, and settle on the models that resonate for you. Ask your peers in other companies what tools they are using. And then once you have settled on a set of development tools for you and your organization; go "narrow & deep" rather than "broad & shallow"; learn as much as you can, as you'll need to champion the development initiatives that lay ahead. You should also know that the leadership model and philosophy that works for one budding leader may not work for another. We're all complex, and we're all different.

I want to share with you a few of the leadership development models and tools that have resonated for me as a coach, and whose use continues to have a deep following in organization of all sizes world-wide. The first was *The Five Practices of Exemplary Leaders* by James Kouzes & Barry Posner (Jossey-Bass, 2012). The Sixth Edition of their groundbreaking book, *The Leadership Challenge*, is due out in 2017. If your goal is to lead, motivate, and inspire others, this is the place to start your journey.

Even we "solopreneurs" have teams. In fact, I have a team that is helping me create this book. When I began studying leadership, teambuilding and team dynamics, the work of Patrick Lencioni, author of *The Five Dysfunctions of a Team* (Jossey-Bass, 2002), *Silos, Politics and Turf Wars* (2008), *The Advantage* (2012), and *The Ideal Team Player* (2016) etc. resonated the most for me. If the growth of your business reaches the point that adding staff is essential – you can't do it all by yourself; you'll need a more strategic approach to building a team than asking for referrals, putting an ad on a job board, or hiring your college roommate or little brother. If there is one thing I've learned from consulting and coaching over the years, if your goal is to build the business with a team, and consistently deliver exceptional customer service and experience, you must invest the time and energy upfront to create the right kind of sustainable company culture. Not believing that this is important is a recipe for _____ (fill in the blank).

When it comes to leadership and team behavior, how we build, cultivate, and sustain relationships can be an eye opener. Long days, tight deadlines, the need to collaborate or make a split-second decision, can be a source of never-ending stress or unanticipated friction. Learning about your own personality – It's best to start with you first, and then that of your team, can be the difference between moving forward or getting stopped in your tracks. During my transition into business coaching, the tool that I have found that complemented the Kouzes & Posner and Lencioni models when working with individuals and teams, was the Everything DISC® suite of personality assessments. I have found when my clients learn about their personality preferences, they are able to have better conversations with their managers, peers, and subordinates.

My pursuit into coaching has been a commitment to ongoing professional development. This development has included exposure into areas that now inform the work I am able to do with my clients. I've come to appreciate the study and application of emotional intelligence, neuroscience, and conflict management, just to name a few. I have learned through training and mentoring, methods to work with organizations to eliminate abrasive behavior in the workplace. This work is based on a method developed by Dr. Laura Crawshaw, author of *Taming the Abrasive Manager* (Jossey-Bass, 2007). Conflict in the workplace is another touchy subject. As my work and expertise into managing conflict has deepened, appreciating that we all have a preference for how we engage in the conflict. The tool that I currently use is the Style Matters: The Kraybill Conflict Style Inventory. Like the other previously mentioned tools, this instrument is psychometrically valid and culturally flexible.

I have come to appreciate that while we are complex, the more leaders and teams can learn about themselves and each other, then the path to business success can be just a "little bit" smoother. If you would like to learn more about The Five Practices of Exemplary Leadership® model, The Five Behaviors of a Cohesive Team™ model, The Everything DiSC® suite of assessments, removing abrasive behavior from the workplace, or managing conflict in the workplace, I would like to invite you to request a Strategy Session with me so that we can chat about what your challenges are. There's no obligation, but I guarantee you'll at least come away with a path of action to take. Here's your link: https://my.timetrade.com/book/JXXMC

To your path to business success,

Howard

PS. Volume II is already in the works.

PPS. If you or someone you know is a business owner that leads a team of three (3) or more, and would like to be considered for a guest slot on my Facebook livestream show, Your Success Path "Live" to talk about how you (they) lead, motivate, and inspire others, please use this link to schedule a time to discuss this opportunity: https://my.timetrade.com/book/JXXMC

PPPS. Please visit www.yourpathtosuccess-book.com to listen to the full interviews from my podcast and livestream shows.

ABOUT THE AUTHOR

Howard Fox is a business coach, LinkedIn expert, sought-after speaker, recovering information technology (IT) business consultant, host of Your Success Path "Live" (a live-stream interview show on Facebook), and founder of Fox Coaching, Inc. Howard coaches business owners and entrepreneurs, managers, and teams to lead, motivate, and inspire others. He also has a knack for helping busy professionals learn to use LinkedIn as a professional branding tool to keep in touch with their current connections, and to attract their ideal clients and customers. Howard holds an MA in Organization Development and Leadership from Fielding Graduate U. He is also a graduate of Fielding's Accredited Coach Training Program. He received his undergraduate degree in Psychology and a graduate degree in Public Administration from Wayne State University. Howard lives in Chicago, IL. He is an avid traveler, photographer, and loves to cook for friends.